AW ARRH!

EXPERIENCES IN THE
WOMEN'S LAND ARMY

ELLEN MIST

UNITED WRITERS
Cornwall

UNITED WRITERS PUBLICATIONS LTD
Ailsa, Castle Gate, Penzance, Cornwall.

British Library Cataloguing in Publication Data

A catalogue record for this book is
available from the British Library.

ISBN 1 85200 043 0

164 7 104566 12016

Printed in Great Britain by
United Writers Publications Ltd
Cornwall

In memory of my mother
who inspired the writing of this book.

PREFACE

I was working in a large department store when the Second World War broke out. As girls left to join up and goods disappeared, I became very unsettled. A chance meeting led me to join the Women's Land Army, although it was against the advice of my doctor and family.

Being totally ignorant of farming and not understanding the dialect of the farm workers, I found myself in the most embarrassing and sometimes extremely funny situations. The work was very hard and each new job tested different muscles.

Nevertheless, as I struggled on through the months it all became easier and I found myself enjoying the life. At the end of the first year I had become quite proficient at dairy work and helping with seasonal jobs.

CONTENTS

Chapter One

GREENER THAN GRASS

"Thee'd best luk ut fer thic Katy," said Fred.

"Aw arrh," agreed Bob.

At least I thought he agreed. It was muttered out of the side of his mouth where was stuck an old black pipe which he sucked on noisily from time to time.

They might have been talking Chinese for all I understood. Except for the word Katy, who was she? I was the only female around, although one could be forgiven for thinking otherwise. Enveloped in a large mac, wellington boots and a felt hat which was on the big side and pulled down against the drizzle, any sign of femininity was lost to view.

Fred looked at me, a sly grin on his face. "Ah, 'er'll give 'ee a poke s'now," he said. This time Bob nodded, took off his cap, scratched his head, and put his cap on again, back to front as before.

Determined not to show my ignorance I smiled brightly. That they were enjoying themselves at my expense there was no doubt.

"You can go out with Fred and old Bob," Boss had said. "They'll take you around the farm." So here we were squelching up a muddy track towards the farmyard. My legs were already beginning to ache with the unaccustomed heavy boots and the effort of dragging each foot out of the muck, but I dug my cold hands in my pockets and plodded on. The men didn't seem to notice the weather, which was wet and cold. They wore ancient macs tied around their middles with string, heavy leather boots and leggings and battered caps pulled on back to front. It must have been a custom for I never saw them otherwise and I never discovered why.

'Taking around' had been a quick look at various yards, a barn and several sheds housing farm implements and tractors — also some stables. Then down the road skirting the farmhouse and garden, back over a paddock to the said track which led to the yard. Thus making a circular detour, now we had come through a gate into the yard along two sides of which were doors leading into the cowsheds. At the other end was another gate which was open, and beyond that fields.

A moment later a herd of cows came shoving and pushing their way through the open gateway. I hoped they were all cows! Black and white they were, but no, as more came into the yard I could see that some were white and black, while a few seemed to be all black or all white with an odd splash or two of contrast.

"Thic's er," commented Fred, pointing to an almost all white animal tossing its head and looking wildly around at the rest who kept their distance. The penny dropped. Katy must be one of the cows. Did they all have names then? My only acquaintance with cows before had been a doe-eyed soft brown creature in a child's picture book, called Daisy. Although my family lived in the country and we had to cross a field to the nearest bus stop, if there were any cows around we gave them a wide berth, not knowing if there might be a bull with them or which it would be, anyway.

"Thee's stay put oi'll toi 'er up fust," said Fred. He carried a big stick which he swung round at the other cows so they drew back leaving Katy isolated. Then he quickly opened the cowshed door and urged her in, shutting it behind him shouting "git un ther" all the while.

Bob didn't offer any help but 'stayed put' with me. He took out his pipe, pressed down the contents with his forefinger, replaced it and began to draw. He seemed nervous and like me eyed the now milling cows as they poked each other, with concern. He also had a stick but I didn't and hoped they would not come too near. I wondered about Katy. Why did she seem so wild? And had she been named after Kate in 'The Taming of the Shrew'? Boss, although a seemingly intelligent man, hadn't struck me as a Shakespeare fan! Perhaps his wife was? Later I learned that Katy had been 'bought in' for her milk yield and probably sold on account of her temperament which hadn't been mentioned at the sale.

Fred reappeared, opened the doors and began letting in the other cows a few at a time. "Bide ther mide," said Bob kindly as I was wondering if I was supposed to help. "Thee's luk tudee." I'd had to guess the meaning of their words and stayed where I was, hoping it was right. As the cows went in I couldn't help thinking of 'the animals went in two by two'. But with Fred and Bob leaping around brandishing their sticks at the others in turn and yelling "Ut thic way Coostard," and "Dang thee oies' Primrose," it wasn't anything like a dignified progress into the Ark but more like a scene from a Western.

How did they remember which were Custard and Primrose? The cows all looked similar to me. The rest seemed to have equally peculiar names, not a Daisy among them. I wondered whose choice it was and if there was a reason, what it could be? Maybe Custard gave thick yellow milk? Subsequently this proved entirely wrong, Friesian milk being almost white. At the far end of the yard another chap was bringing in a few stragglers. He let them in the sheds opposite and disappeared: "George sids to thic uns," said Fred.

They had now dealt with all the cows. I walked over and glanced through the doors. They were all tied up with chains round their necks, two to a stall, munching some hay which was in the cribs in front of them. The floor was cemented with a step down behind them onto a gangway which had a gutter at the back. A sprinkling of straw was spread along under the cows' front legs.

Boss had come into the shed by another door at the end. "Come down to the house for a cup of tea and a milking apron," he said. I joined him. On the way he showed me the dairy at the end of the shed. He explained about the milking machine, heavy buckets with rubber teats hanging from their lids and rubber tubes twisted in a coil on top. They looked very complicated to me. There was also a cooling system consisting of a small tank with a tap, positioned over a corrugated hollow galvanised iron cooler. It had a tray at the bottom with a funnel in the middle. A churn was placed under this which had a filter over the top. Water ran from a tap into the cooler by a pipe at one side and out the other. There was also a sterilising cabinet and a large galvanised tank with hot and cold water. At that time it was all very modern, although I didn't realise it then. I was wondering how it all worked, including getting the milk from the cows with the six milkers and if I would have to cope with them.

We walked back to the house and took off our boots and macs in the passage. Missus had made a cup of tea in the kitchen. I needed something, what with the weather, the unfamiliar language of Fred and Bob, cows which had temperaments — *all*. Plus the sight of the various contraptions

14

in the dairy. I felt entirely out of my element.

The tea did nothing to restore me. It was weak and there was no sugar. Never having had it without before I thought it awful. Although sugar was rationed we'd always had a little in our tea at home. I hadn't meant to, but I must have made a face as Missus said that we couldn't have cakes if we had sugar in tea. She produced some home-made biscuits which compensated a bit. I said I expected I'd soon get used to it and eventually I did, never liking sugar in tea again.

"We'd better move," said Boss. Missus brought out the milking aprons. They were white gowns which enveloped me completely, and while Boss had a white round hat there was a cotton square for me to tie around my head. Dressed in these outfits we looked fit for any operating theatre!

Back at the dairy, George was taking two of the milkers over to the other cowshed. He was also clad in white. Bob was struggling into similar garb but kept on his cap. Presumably he took it off for bed but apart from removing it now and then to scratch his head, I never saw him without it. It was always the same old battered one, even on a Sunday. There was no sign of Fred. It seemed Boss did the milking in one shed aided by Bob who then had to go over and help George finish the other lot. I was to learn to replace Bob (with Boss) so that he could help George at the start and so speed it all up. "We still have to milk a few by hand," said Boss, "so you could try old Custard, she's quiet, while we get on with the machine." He gave me a bucket and three legged stool, pointed to a cow at the bottom of the shed and went back to fixing up the first ones with the milking machine buckets. I stared at the cow in dismay. She had a big udder with large triangular teats practically touching the ground. How on earth did one get the milk out? No wonder she had to be hand milked. A machine would never get anywhere near that lot. Bob came along carrying a bucket and stool.

"Them's no' ready fer oi yet, oi'll shoo'ee mide." So saying he went up to Custard and patted her. Then he straddled the stool alongside the cow and tilted the bucket practically on its side between his legs and started to milk, while I watched. It looked easy.

"Ready for stripping," called Boss and Bob got up.

"Av tu git them drips," he said, "Yu 'av a go." He went off to strip out the last drops of milk from the cows after Boss took off the milking buckets.

There was no putting off the evil hour. I now had to try my hand at milking. Custard looked round as I made to start, decided I wasn't worth a second glance and went on munching hay. I sat down as Bob had shown me but was not able to get the bucket in position without a lot of clatter. The cow took no notice so I gingerly reached out to clutch her nearest teats. I tried pulling gently and squeezing but not a drop of milk appeared. Perhaps there wasn't any left in these two? I tried to reach under her to the others. I couldn't even get hold of them — they were too far away. Bob came back to see how I was getting on.

"She doesn't seem to have any milk left," I said, hoping it was true.

Bob shook his head, "Must 'ave, oi' only tuk a drip."

My heart sank, "I can't get any out," I sighed. Up the other end Boss was ready again.

"Luk 'ere," Bob said, holding up his hands half closed and then gradually lowered them with a clenching movement, "Troi it." He left. I started again. I could only get my hands half way round her teats anyway as they were so big. Imitating Bob's method I stroked and squeezed. A few drops of milk appeared — ah success! But after five minutes I still only had a little milk in the bucket and hadn't managed the steady stream that I'd seen Bob producing. My hands were

16

aching, and my back where I was nearly bent double to reach Custard's udder. She was evidently fed up with my amateur efforts as well and gave me a slap round my face with her dirty tail. I got up. I was never going to be a milkmaid that was for sure.

Bob reappeared, "Dun 'ee mine," he said, "oi'll du'er. Thee's'll larn."

"Do you really think so?" I asked doubtfully.

"Aw arrh." Bob nodded. He finished off Custard and stripped a couple of other cows which Boss had ready. He had milked all of them by this time and was taking off the buckets at my end.

"How are you getting on then?" he asked.

I explained I hadn't been able to get the knack of milking.

"Never mind Custard's a bit low. You can try stripping tomorrow, you might get the hang of it then," he said. Bob was taking his bucket and stool back to the dairy. We followed. Boss carried two milking buckets full of milk. He tipped it up to be cooled and changed the churn underneath, which was full as were several others.

While I'd been dawdling with Custard, Boss and George had milked sixty-odd cows with the machine buckets. Bob had stripped most of them and George the rest. Boss showed me how to wash up all the dairy things, cold water first. Then hot with a sterilising solution added. The actual sterilising cabinet was only used once a day in the mornings. Then all the machine was taken to pieces, thoroughly washed with the rest and put in the chest and sterilised with steam.

Meanwhile, Bob and George were letting the cows out into the yard and from there to the field. Then they came back to the dairy and took off their milking aprons and went home. Having washed up Boss and I did the same. We no longer looked like potential surgeons. Our aprons were streaked with cow muck and my face was also well plastered. We

17

walked back to the farmhouse where Missus had high tea ready. After a wash and a good meal I went up to unpack my clothes as I was going to 'live in'.

It was only a few hours since I had met Boss in my local country town and travelled the twenty-odd miles to the farm. It seemed a lifetime ago. I sat on the bed feeling very tired and mused on how it had all come about.

Chapter Two

BEWITCHED, BOTHERED AND BEWILDERED

I had been unable to follow a career of my choice owing to family circumstances and I was working in a big department store in my local town. There was plenty of scope for promotion, but one had to start at the bottom to learn all about the business and work in the various departments in turn.

I was getting on quite well and a few steps up the ladder when the Second World War came. At first it made very little difference but gradually things changed. Goods began to get short and some lines became unobtainable. The manager joined the army and an older man took his place. Girls left to join the forces or go into reserved jobs. The first floor was closed down and all the business concentrated on the ground floor.

There was not any joy in going to work. With a shortage of goods and staff, customers became grumpy and awkward. As we lived in the country I had a six mile cycle ride to work. When the air-raids started the store began closing at 6.00 pm instead of the usual 7.30 pm weekdays, 8.00 pm Friday and 9.00 pm Saturday. Wednesday stayed early closing day at 1.00 pm. The idea was that staff should get home before the siren which regularly went off just after

6.00 pm. I was still on my way home and felt very nervous until I heard the planes go over and the all-clear sounded. Normally they were on route to another destination. Once they dropped some incendiaries on the town causing a few fires. Later on a land mine dropped near my home.

One evening in the late summer, I returned home to find we had a visitor — a young woman I had not seen before, or so I thought. She was in a fawn Aertex shirt with a green pullover, corduroy breeches and had on long socks with brown shoes. A felt hat was tilted on one side of her head. I wondered if she was having riding lessons locally, as I sometimes saw people out on horses when I was cycling along the lane.

"You don't remember me, do you?" she said.

I replied that I hadn't a clue. She said that she had been a friend of my sister at school. There was now no resemblance to the cheeky seven-year-old as I had last seen her. She and my sister had always been getting into mischief, ending with us all in trouble. I'd been glad when the family moved away. Later we also moved several times. Such is chance that we should meet again so many years after. The result was to change my whole life.

She told us that she had recently joined the Women's Land Army and was living in a hostel with several other girls a few miles away. They travelled around to local farms where they were short handed to help with seasonal work, as many men had been called up in the forces. She said it was just about a good life. They had been haymaking in lovely weather and it was fun. She certainly looked tanned and healthy. In the evenings they went out to the pictures in the nearest town or dances with the local lads who were left.

She had heard that we were living in the area and this being her day off she decided to pay us a visit. We had never heard of the WLA but as she went on about the free uniform, meals and pay, it sounded a delightful way to earn a living. She left and promised to keep in touch, but we didn't see her again.

Months went by and as winter came the journeys from work became a nightmare. Having to cycle with practically no light (only a glimmer was allowed), along dark country lanes with planes zooming overhead was no fun. I frequently hit a stone and fell off or had to walk if the surface was slippery with frost or snow. It was hard weather and I often thought of the idealistic life of our friend in the WLA, not realising that it would be very different at this time of the year.

In the spring I became more unsettled. Most of my friends at the store had already left, being replaced by younger or older married women. There was not much to sell in any case. I would have joined up, but the family would not hear of a suggestion to go in the forces and parents permission for girls under twenty-one had to be obtained, and at twenty-one I would be drafted into essential war work.

I decided to find out about the WLA. There seemed to be no difficulty. A doctor's certificate of fitness was required and references of background and character. Already I was savouring the delights of life ahead in the sun and fresh air.

The first snag occurred when I saw my family doctor to obtain the required medical certificate. He was a big jovial man and when I stated the purpose of my visit he hooted with laughter and then stared at me in disbelief. I assured him I was serious in my intention to join the WLA. "Well, my dear," he said, "I must say I think you look too fragile. My own daughter works in it and she would make two of you. However, I'll give you a thorough examination." This done, he told me I was perfectly fit and he would give me the certificate but he added: "I wouldn't advise you to do farm work. However, if you really want to, take it easy for a while and of course you can always leave it if it's too much for you."

I was not a bit put off by any of this. Rather the opposite. Still seeing our friend's picturesque description of life on the land, I was determined to try it. I didn't think that our doctor could really know and thought he was just pessimistic. Likewise the family, who gave me a few weeks at the most. So it came about that one lunchtime I was met by the local organiser of the WLA who was going to introduce me to my future employer. Being market day he would be coming to town for business. It had all been arranged that, subject to interview, I would go to his farm to help generally and live in. This was a rather different arrangement from the friend's, but it was considered more suitable for myself and at least the family were happier about it.

Boss, as he was known to me after, arrived at the meeting place. He didn't seem very impressed with my looks either. I was slim with a pink and white complexion which I suppose must have made me look delicate in comparison to the 'Missus', whom he had brought with him. She was tall and hefty, with rosy cheeks and her hair pulled back in a bun under a felt hat. A tweed coat and brogues completed the picture. After remarking that I didn't look very strong they decided that anyway I could come for a month on trial.

I could have a weekend off every other one as I wasn't used to farm work and I'd probably need it. As I had to give notice at the store they would collect me in two weeks at the same place.

By this time I was thoroughly fed up with everyone's assumption that I was not suitable for my proposed occupation. Secretly, I was a little worried but I decided I'd show them all and nothing nor nobody would make me change my mind. I gave in my notice and during the following days my determination grew. A few friends that were left obviously thought me quite mad. They would rather be drafted to a munitions factory, but that prospect horrified me and I knew I'd made the right decision. The deputy manager wished me luck but seemed uninterested. He had enough of his own problems and another person leaving added to them.

In the meantime I arranged to collect my uniform from the organiser who obtained the items from the headquarters in London. These comprised of one pair of khaki corduroy breeches, two fawn poplin shirts, a green pullover, two pairs of long fawn socks and one pair of brown leather brogues. There was also a donkey brown short overcoat and felt hat, wellingtons, a heavy mac, two pairs of fawn dungarees, black boots and a short twill cotton jacket and two Aertex shirts.

In those days very few girls wore trousers but with a clothes and stockings shortage many were beginning to. Also for taking on men's jobs they were far more serviceable. I hadn't any myself and breeches were my first experience. I thought them ghastly when I tried on the uniform. Being new they were fairly stiff and with laces to tie in around the calf, plus long socks on top, one felt stuffed up. Adding heavy shoes to slim feet and the velour coat weighing down my shoulders it seemed an effort to get around. All were very good quality, however, and obviously made to last — longer than me perhaps! No wonder they wanted stalwarts! It required energy just to carry the garb for the job! Anyway, I assumed one would not wear the coat for working which would lighten things a bit.

On reflection, which of it all would one work in? Our friend had been off duty when we saw her and clad in the first mentioned items. Surely they would get dirty if worn around the farm? The dungarees, of course, they would be for work. But although it was March, winter was still around with cold winds and icy showers. It would need sweated labour to keep warm in those. Sweated labour? Oh dear? Maybe I was a lamb going to the slaughter! That was a thought − would there be any lambs? I was to help with the cows and learn milking. There'd been no mention of sheep or lambs. In any case, they would have a shepherd, or would they?

As the time came nearer for me to go, I grew more and more apprehensive. What if everyone else was right and I was hopeless, not strong enough, not know what to wear for the best, not have a clue about cows? It didn't add up to a happy conclusion. Was I being pig-headed? Pigs? How about them? *How about them?* Farms sometimes kept pigs − I knew that. My knowledge was limited to the vaguely remembered pigs in a sty at the bottom of our garden, on one place where we had lived, when I was a small child. They had grunted a lot and ate everything in sight. One had always been killed for the house, but on that day we children had to make ourselves scarce. We hadn't been allowed, nor wanted, to be there. It had been bad enough to hear the squeals a long way off. I had hated the scalding and smoking smells as it was prepared. It had been difficult to fancy any of it, and I only had ever liked the liver. However, one was told to 'eat up and be thankful' in those days, and we weren't allowed to be choosey.

There had also been hens kept in a run; we children thought they were silly things which made a great fuss if our puppy went near. He would follow us as we walked alongside to reach the grassed part of the garden where we played. Headed by a magnificent bronze cockerel, the hens would leap at the wire flapping their wings and squawking their heads off. Whereupon we would get a telling off, while the pup hid behind us. No, I didn't want to look after poultry either. I consoled myself with the thought that maybe they wouldn't keep pigs or poultry, or, if they did, someone else would look after them.

It just depended how long it took to do whatever had to be done with the cows. Boss had said "cows, milking and generally useful" so I might have to do anything after that. It was no use wondering and worrying. I would just have to wait and see. After all, I was only going on a month's trial and I would have a weekend off after two weeks. I could try it. Boss might not want me after that and I might not want to stay. All the same, a month seemed a long time.

On the appointed day I dressed in the uniform. It really was quite smart but I felt very conscious of people's stares as, with my suitcase, I caught the bus to town. I suppose hardly anyone had seen a woman from the Land Army. In comparison to the other forces they were very thin on the ground and widely scattered. I left the bus and walked to the market. It was time to meet Boss and his wife. My new life was about to begin.

Chapter Three

COWS BUT NOT COMMON

When I was at home, I cycled along the lanes to work every day. If it was my half day off I would walk across the fields to catch the bus on the main road to town, to go shopping or to the pictures or to meet a friend. I was doing this now but it was different. However much I tried to walk I stayed in the same place as my feet were heavy and wouldn't move. I was halfway across the first meadow where there were usually some cows lying down or munching grass well away from the footpath. This time they were all coming towards me, black and white, with lowered heads. I felt panicky! I couldn't move! They would knock me down! Then someone was calling them back with a piercing shriek. I woke up. It was the sound of an alarm and I'd been having a nightmare.

Although I was glad to be awake and find it only a dream, for a few minutes I couldn't think where I was. This was a strange bed in a strange room. Memory came back. I was starting a new life on a farm. I looked at the clock — only 6 am. I knew I'd have to get up. It had been agreed on the night before. I wasn't used to rising before 7.30 am. That's why I'd had to set the alarm. The air felt cold and I longed to snuggle down again under the bedclothes. It was no good.

With an effort I got out of bed. Now then, what to wear? I decided on the dungarees, although new, they weren't as stiff as the breeches and felt more comfortable. I'd have to chance being too cold. I arrived in the kitchen; Boss was already there. We had tea and a biscuit. Then into the milking aprons and out up to the cowsheds.

Bob and George were bringing in the cows and I was asked to help tie them up as they came into the shed, a few at a time. They knew their places, surprising me. Keeping well away from Katy's end, I gingerly went to tie one up. She was interested in a bit of hay in the crib and took little notice of me, so, growing confident, I tied up several more. When they were all in it was the same routine as the afternoon before. This morning, however, they were all given a bowl or two of cow cake before being milked, according to how much they gave. Boss explained how the milk was weighed and recorded once a week, morning and evening, and their rations worked out. A lady came from the Milk Marketing Board to do it. It seemed that there was a lot more to producing milk than met the eye or should it be udder!

"You can try a bit of stripping," said Boss. "Just use your fingers and thumb." He pointed to a long legged animal from which he'd just taken off the machine. I picked up my bucket and stool and went to sit and have a go. In complete contrast to old Custard of my previous day's effort, this one's teats were small and high up. I twiddled about and a few drops of milk popped in the empty bucket. A few more and then she moved forward putting her near hind leg right in front of her udder. She'd decided she'd had enough. I didn't know what to do now. Bob came along.

"Owz it mide?" I got up and shook my head. "Old 'ard Coostard me 'ole gal," he said, and shoving his shoulder under her leg deftly moved it back. He turned to me. "Thic's 'ow 'ee doos 'un."

27

Had I heard right? Bob calling this cow Custard? Surely there weren't two? Ah! Maybe he couldn't remember their names, so he called them all the same! I had another go at stripping her. The same thing happened again so I shoved my shoulder under her leg as Bob had showed me. She moved it back then wham! She kicked the bucket. I managed to stop it tipping over. There was still very little milk in it anyway. I felt shaken. What had I done different from Bob? Of course! I hadn't said "old 'ard me 'ole gal," whatever that meant. The cow looked around and tossed her head. 'That's for you,' she seemed to say. 'You'd better learn to talk nicely to a lady before you take liberties with her legs.' Hearing the clatter Boss had come up.

"She's not usually fidgety," he said. "I expect she knows you're fresh." Then looking in the bucket, "That's about all you'll get. You can strip Dainty and Primrose along there now; they are very quiet." But what if they also knew I was fresh and decided to show me what they could do? I'd better be on the safe side and tip out the little milk I had into the collecting bucket behind.

There'd been no need to wonder if I'd be warm. The heat from the cows and being scared was enough. I was sweating like a bull. Did bulls sweat? Were there any on the farm and if so where? I hadn't heard anything about them so far. Banish the thought. Cows were enough at the moment. I wasn't doing very well with them.

I got on better with Primrose who had even teats about the right height and the milk came out easily. Dainty wasn't too bad either. I began to feel better. Then Boss said, "That's the lot, come along to the dairy." My heart sank. I'd only stripped three cows while Bob must have milked four by hand and stripped a dozen. "Nearly 8 o'clock," said Boss. "The lorry will be here any minute." We'd been in the cowstall getting on for two hours. It hadn't seemed that

28

long although I felt hungry. The full churns of milk were put out on the stand and all the milking utensils rinsed in cold water. Bob, George and Fred had let out the cows and went off for their breakfast. Boss showed me how to take the milking machine to bits, wash it all thoroughly in hot soda water and then put it in the steriliser. This took quite some time and I was longing for something to eat. At last all was done. The milk lorry arrived and collected the milk. Boss and I went down to the house for a substantial meal.

There was porridge, something I was not very fond of, but, being hungry enough, it went down well with milk and a little golden syrup. Then eggs, home produced. There were hens somewhere then? Yes, Missus kept them in the paddock near the house. We finished with toast, butter and home-made jam. There was always milk and butter. Pans of milk were set to take off the cream and make it each week. The skimmed milk was used for bread puddings, the rest went to a man who kept pigs nearby. There were none on the farm.

During the meal I asked Boss about the cows' names. He explained these were no ordinary animals. They had family trees! In other words pedigrees. I knew that some dogs had them, but cows! Boss told me that there were several generations in the herd and like kings and queens they were called after their ancestors. Some were the first or second and so on, but others were named like the Custard family. Old Custard, Young Custard, Little Custard and Baby Custard, very confusing, especially when the adjectives ran out. Then they were called by something supposed to be similar. The latest Muffett was named Powder Puff. I really couldn't see the connection. Bob had been right then calling several Custard but he knew them all. I wondered if I ever would, even if I'd be there long enough? Still, Rome wasn't built in a day and there was a month to go.

After breakfast I was to help Bob clean out the cowsheds and feed the calves. They had to be fed first. There was some milk in the dairy which had been saved for the very small ones. Bob made it warm with a little hot water. He put some in each of the two buckets and trudged over to the calf pens, me following. As he opened the door of the first one, six calves noses pushed out. Shoving four aside he let two of them nuzzle into the buckets. They slurped up the milk noisily. Meantime the others were sucking and pulling his coat from behind. "Ut thic wye," he said giving them some elbow, but they took no notice.

It took two more journeys to feed the other four then he started on the older ones. They had a bought 'calf weaner mixture' which had to be made up and resembled milk. It followed the same pattern — two fed at a time while the others made themselves a nuisance. Lastly, the biggest calves had to have water carried and put in troughs in their pens. This wasn't the end by any means. There was a load of hay in a shed nearby. Bob carried flaps of it on a prong for all the calves and plonked it in the racks in the pens. The oldest ones also were given some home mixed meal concentrate. All the time the ones waiting to be fed bawled their heads off. "Ush up noisy varmits," Bob shouted to all and sundry, but he might as well have saved his breath. They continued to kick up a row until it was their turn to be fed.

All this time I'd just tracked around after Bob and tried to take in which was given what. I needn't have bothered, the calves were Bob's babies. Although I was supposed to help him and share all the work, after the first day he invariably left me to get on with cleaning out the sheds while he did all the calf feeding. I got the impression that he didn't think I could cope with them. I was quite sure I couldn't.

"We'm 'ull sid to thim bulls now," said Bob as we were making our way back to the cowsheds. He took out his pipe and grunted. I didn't say anything but he knew I was scared. Where were they? "Yu tak a poke o'ay in ther," he said, pointing to a shed and giving me his prong. "Oi'll git sim water."

I looked at him in disbelief. Surely he didn't mean me to go in the shed with a bull.

It seemed he did. "Ers toid up," Bob said and, picking up two buckets, walked off. Evidently his kindness to me with the cows in the milking shed didn't apply when it came to feeding bulls. Oh well, I supposed I could only get killed?

Knees shaking, I went over to the hayshed and pronged a heap of hay. I managed to carry it without dropping too much. Gingerly I opened the bull pen door. A snorting met my ears. As I gazed in, an enormous bull turned its head and bellowed. It was worse than I thought.

" 'Ers a nasty un," said Bob behind me. "Kip in thic soid." He was carrying two buckets of water, "Git un," he went on.

I had no choice. I 'gitted un', 'kipped to thic soid' and poked the hay in front of the bull. As he started to eat it Bob nipped up and put the buckets where he could drink from them. Then we both got out of the door quickly. Although I was feeling like a jelly I could see Bob wasn't too happy either. Was he scared too? It seemed like it.

"T'other's mun so bad," Bob said now. Indeed when we fed and watered the older bull he seemed quite docile. Even so, I'd had enough of bulls and felt thankful to still be alive. At last we went over to make a start on cleaning out the cowsheds.

Armed with brushes and shovels we had to load up the dung into a wheelbarrow and wheel it outside over the yard and through a door to a large heap. I scraped more up

31

together while Bob trundled the loads away. "Bist tricky mide," Bob said. "Thic barrer will tip any ole ow." I had no ambition to try it. I was already tired and aching with the brushing and shovelling.

Now and again Bob stopped and relit his pipe or took off his cap, scratched his head and put it back on while he leaned on the shovel. I leaned on mine too and tried to make a little conversation but I didn't get very far, only some 'aw arrhs' and a few other words I didn't understand.

After the muck had been all cleared out we had to wash down and scrub the sheds with brooms until all was clean. At least there were some hoses in the big sheds. Later in some smaller ones we had to carry buckets of water from a trough. When all was done Bob said, "Speck tiz time for vittels." He pulled a pocket watch out of his waistcoat pocket. "Aw arrh, tiz, ai be orf," so saying as he went.

I supposed I had better go back to the house, and sure enough Boss was already in. Over dinner he asked me how I had got on. I said I didn't think I'd done too badly.

"I expect Bob scared you over the bulls didn't he?" asked Boss.

I admitted as much.

"They are not really as bad as they seem," he said. "The young ones are a bit lively but you needn't take much notice of the noise they make, doesn't mean anything. Bob's got it in his head that they're wild and dangerous and is frightened to death of them. I let him go on tending to them as I know they're safe enough tied up."

"I see," I said. Actually I felt in sympathy with Bob. They had sounded wild and dangerous to me and I wasn't really reassured by Boss's remarks.

After dinner, George came round and Boss told him to take me with him mending fences. Although he was the cowman, he didn't do any cleaning out, only on a Sunday when everyone helped with the milking and routine jobs so that they could finish early and have the rest of the day off.

George had a couple of rolls of barbed wire to carry so he gave me the bag of tools. We walked down the road to some meadows and through the gate. We had to go round and check that all the fences were stockproof before any animals could be put there. Here and there wire was down and I handed George staples with which he nailed it up again. In some places it was broken so he cut it off and put in new pieces. It was quite good to be doing nothing much. After the strenuous morning my arms, back and legs were aching and handing over a few nails was easy. George didn't say much and he definitely had an accent but at least I could understand what he did say, unlike the other two, when I just guessed at their meaning.

After a couple of hours, however, and having been round three fields, I was cold with standing around and bored stiff. There was a nippy wind and George's conversation was very limited. I was glad when he said that we'd better go back and get the cows in as it was nearly milking time.

This time I helped him take the cows from the field back to the farm. They had to be called out, "Kup, kup cum un." I wondered who originated these words. Anyway they knew and 'cummed in'. I went in front along the road to open the yard gate — George brought up the rear — Bob was in the yard and we got them tied up. I recognised Katy and kept out of her way. Also, after a good look at her teats I knew Old Custard. It seemed possible now that I might in time know them all.

Boss appeared and we went into the house for a cuppa. Then it was the same routine as the previous afternoon except that I did manage to strip a couple more cows than before.

When we'd finished and had tea, I felt very tired. I decided

33

to have a hot bath and go to bed early. It had been quite a day.

Chapter Four

THE DAILY ROUND

The next morning when I awoke I could hardly move. I was stiff and aching all over. As I got up to dress all my muscles protested.

I thought back to my school days. After the holidays, the first gym lesson used to leave me much the same. Would I feel better as the day went on?

Over the morning cup of tea Boss said, "I expect you'll find the work a bit hard at first, as you're not used to it. Get old Bob to do the heaviest." I was wondering if I'd get through the milking, let alone any more work. My hands and fingers were aching along with the rest of me.

The morning routine was the same. In the cowshed I struggled on, stripping a few cows, then there was washing up and breakfast. After that I went to help Bob. No use saying to Bob what Boss had said — Bob went off to his calves and left me to do most of the cleaning, wheeling out the muck and washing down on my own. He said we'd get the work done quicker that way and who was I to argue? He'd been there years and I was only on my second day. At least I'd not have to face the bulls.

He turned up when it was nearly all done. By this time I was fit to drop. He did wheel out the last barrow. I'd left it and gone on washing down. I could see I was going to have to be a bit crafty like him.

Dinner-time was a welcome respite. After there was more fencing, giving my aching limbs a rest. Then the milking again, tea and finish. Too tired to do anything but wash and look at the paper, I felt very dispirited.

The days went slowly by. Every one the same and I had to keep on, my body protesting all the time. I moaned about it to George but got short shrift from him. "You'll get used to it. Come haymaking time you'll be jolly glad to come in and do the milking," was all he said.

There was worse to come then, and how long was it before that, I asked.

"Oh, June maybe, depends on the weather," he replied.

It was only March now. Would I stick it for three months and why would haymaking be so dreadful. I thought of the friend who'd lured me into this life with her enthusiasm. She'd liked haymaking so she said, but she hadn't had to get used to milking and mucking out. She'd lived in a hostel with other girls and went out doing seasonal jobs. Maybe they were given the easier work or didn't do much? They were, anyway, on a five day week.

The milk recorder came in the week, which made a little change and it was interesting to note the different yields of milk from each cow.

I was to learn that freshly calved cows gave several gallons a day and it very slowly became less during the months until they were dried off for a few weeks before having the next calf. The other facts of a cow's life I didn't discover until later on.

The weekend was a welcome relief. Only the milking had to be done on Saturday afternoon and on Sunday the milking, mucking out and feeding of the calves. Fred came in to help and with Boss, George, Bob and me, we soon got through it all. I had to do my washing and keep my room clean so it wasn't all rest, but I could relax and there was time to take a walk around the village and have a look at the locals. The nearest town was three miles away and I didn't go far that first weekend.

The next week followed the same pattern varying sometimes in the afternoons. On a wet day there was cow meal to be ground and mixed in the barns. Slabs of linseed and cotton-cake were fed into a grinder which was turned by hand handle and hard work it was. This was mixed with rolled oats and sugarbeet pulp in proportion to make a balanced feed. It had to be mixed on the floor and shovelled into bags. Or I would have to help George and Bob spring cleaning the cowsheds. This was in addition to the daily cleaning and done once a year in the spring when the weather did not permit much work outside.

Dust and cobwebs had to be got down from the roof and walls. Then the walls, which were richly decorated with muck, had to be scrubbed down with buckets of hot soda water. After that we had to clean all the cribs where the cows had their food, the doors, partitions and 'tie ups'. Then the wooden partitions and doors had to be creosoted. I had this job while the others whitewashed the roofs and walls. However, as it was done over a period of time, at each session we had to do some cleaning again and it was some weeks later that we finished.

One evening Boss said we were going to have another girl to help. She didn't belong to the WLA but lived locally. She'd been used to riding and working with horses on weekends and was too young to be called up but wanted a job on a farm. He thought we girls could have alternate weekends off. Also have a week on and a week off dairy work. Alternately working in the fields where there would be an increasing amount to do as the year went on.

So Margaret arrived and a week later I had my first week-end off. After Saturday lunch I caught the bus at the end of the lane and sighed with relief as I sank into a seat. No more work for nearly two days.

At home the time passed very quickly. Everything was fine I assured them and didn't say anything about my aches and pains or my trials with the cows. Not for anything would I admit that it was all very different from what I'd expected. Soon it was Sunday morning and time to go back to the farm. I had to leave early as there were no late buses.

Margaret, living near, had been home some of the day. Our rooms led into each other so we were able to chat. It was nice having another girl. She was rather casual and said and did the funniest things without realising it, with me then getting the giggles. It was to brighten things up no end.

Not belonging to the WLA, at first Margaret put on her riding gear for work. Very classy it was. She looked as if she were off to a hunt. However, after a few encounters with cow muck she wisely bought some dungarees, although she continued to wear her silk shirts. We both had to help with the milking in the morning but now, after breakfast, she was to do the dairy and help Bob, while I went on field work for a week and then we would change over again.

Although there were two tractors which Boss and Fred drove, some of the work was still done with horses. Jack the carter had charge of these and on my first week out I was told to go with him. At first, as with the cows, I was totally ignorant of horses, and although in time I became good with cows and attached to them, I never got very far or felt the same about horses. However, Margaret was in her element when it was her turn.

On reaching the stables Jack and I went in. There were two horses munching hay — Jack said their names were Punch and Judy. He harnessed up Punch, muttering away.

I presumed he was explaining about the gear as he then told me to have a go with Judy. I was hopeless: lifting the collar off the wall I sank under the weight and dropped it. Judy gave a snort of disgust and kicked up her heels. Jack was grinning, "Leave 'er be," he said. He picked up the collar and put it back. " 'Ers a bit loivly, we dun wan 'er anyways."

I was already by the door ready for flight. So he'd done it on purpose. I decided to ignore him. He led Punch round to the cart shed, me following. There he hitched him to a wagon. Fred came round and they loaded up a plough. Jack and I climbed on the wagon and we went off to an arable field where we were going to work. Jack told me we were going to plough some furrows for potato planting.

It was some distance away from the farm and when we arrived Fred was already there having driven the tractor and a trailer with the potatoes and buckets. They unloaded the plough and Jack unhitched Punch from the wagon and hitched him into the traces of the plough. He set it into position to cross the middle of the field. I was to lead the horse while he guided the plough and Fred was to drop the potatoes from a bucket at intervals.

"Let's git goin'," said Jack. I picked up Punch's halter to lead him but he had other ideas. He strode forward and it was wrenched from my hand. He was off, the plough slithering across the ground.

"Woa theese girt varmit," shouted Jack, "Woa-oah."

Fred laughed, but he ran and caught hold of the halter and backed him while Jack reversed the plough. "Theese mus tak tu 'im loike," said Jack.

Ruefully looking at my sore hand I would have liked to more than talk to him. However, I gingerly approached with a "Good boy then." I sounded daft but it seemed to do the trick as he stood still this time and we waited.

There was a "Git im," from Jack. The horse knew the

signal and we went. It seemed he was more leading me than the other way. At a "Wug un" or a "Wug orf" from Jack he pulled either to the left or right. So I did too. He understood what it meant which I certainly didn't, never having heard anything like it before. We reached the other side of the field, leaving, to my surprise, a reasonably straight furrow behind. We turned and waited for Fred to finish dropping the potatoes. Then we set off on a returning journey so that the next furrow covered the potatoes. After this we worked the other side of the row and then back around the same side again and so on. A bit later Fred and Jack decided it was break time.

Squatting in the hedge Fred pulled out an ancient pipe and filled it from a tin of tobacco then handed some to Jack who proceeded to roll it in cigarette papers he had in his pocket. He supplied the matches and they lit up and sighed with satisfaction. Smoking wasn't really allowed on the farm although Bob always had a pipe, even if only sucking on it and keeping it out of sight when Boss was around. It seemed a case of what the eye didn't see.

I sat down as well. I'd worn wellingtons but being a nice spring day my feet were hot and I was glad to take off my jumper.

Then it was back to work after Jack had finished his fag. It seemed hours later but it was only twelve o'clock when Jack consulted his pocket watch and announced dinnertime. We'd planted about a third of the field in the middle. There would be kale one end and mangolds the other, Fred told me. It seemed a queer plan. I hadn't heard anything about rotation of crops.

After dinner I was sent to help Bob in the garden. I decided to wear the black boots we'd been issued with. On Boss's advice I'd rubbed them well with dubbin to soften the leather but they still felt stiff and heavy. It was an effort to walk about.

I had to rake over the ground which Bob had dug while he went on with the next patch. Reaching out with the rake my feet didn't co-ordinate and down I went. I picked myself up — Bob had come over. " 'Ere mide I'll shoo'ee." He took the rake and with nice steady strokes pulled and pushed it over the soil. It looked easy. I tried again and managed a bit better. It was hard work though and I was glad to finish. But that was not all! We had to drag a stone roller over it. Then it had to be raked again and rolled once more. " 'Twill mak a fain bid," said Bob. I could have done with lying on one right then!

However, it seemed it was time to help with the cows. George and Margaret had got them in. We made our way to the sheds, my boots clonking at every step. After our pre-milking cuppa I changed back into wellingtons for milking. There was already a blister on my ankle. That was the end of boots as far as I was concerned. In future I would wear the shoes we had which were meant to be worn with our going out uniform. Not that I'd had much time and energy so far for any social life.

Next day I again had to help in the garden. There were the potatoes to put in and seeds to plant. This was a much nicer job, I enjoyed the warm sunshine and it seemed there might be something to be said for land work, after all. I wore my shoes and although heavy they didn't seem so bad. However, I still had sore heels and toes. Evening found me bathing them and rubbing in surgical spirit. "Will harden them off," said Missus. She didn't seem to have much time for us girls, but was practically kind. Used to hard work and helping outside herself at times, she obviously thought us softies.

Other field jobs followed. The one I hated most was stone picking. I was usually on my own and had to go over a big field with a bucket picking up stones and dumping them in the gateway to fill in pot holes. Then the field could be rolled and left for grass or cultivation without damaging the machinery. Spring was the time for all these activities and Boss and Fred were out on the tractors all day and evening as it grew lighter.

Sometimes now in the evening Margaret and I would get on our bikes and cycle into town to her home or to the pictures. I was settling down and except on a fresh job my muscles ached less as they became accustomed to work.

Came the end of the month, Boss said he thought I would do and I could stay on if I liked. I wasn't all that keen but I was still determined not to give in and admit I couldn't stick being a land girl, so I agreed to stay. After all, one had to do something and everyone said the war would not last much longer. How little they knew.

Chapter Five

NUTS IN MAY

One day Boss said we were going to start turning out the calves. They had been kept in sheds all the winter but were gradually to be let out to grass. The oldest batch would be taken to a field which had a covered yard at the end, then they could be allowed out for a little while at a time, until they were used to it. Otherwise too much grass at once would upset them. There would still be hay available. They were housed in sheds around a big yard which had a barn one end and the bulls' sheds at the other, and what a game we had.

Bob opened the pen door. At first nothing happened, then one calf nosed its way forward and out. The next minute they were all tumbling out and galloping around the yard with their tails up. They tossed their heads and bellowed. On hearing this the bulls started roaring away in frustration at not being able to join in. We all kept clear as they continued to tear about. "They'll quieten down," said Boss. "Then we'll move them." Sure enough one after another they stopped as, panting and puffing, they became out of breath. Then they went over to the water trough for a drink and finally stood staring at us as if to say 'what next?'

We were to take them out of a gate at the end of the yard

near the barn, around the road past the farmhouse and into a gate on the road side of the field. Margaret was to open the gate and stand ready to shoo them in. Bob and I were to get them out of the yard with Boss outside to start them in the right direction, then each of us in turn would get ahead to post ourselves in the various openings on the way. It all sounded simple enough. The reality was entirely different: to start with they didn't want to be moved. Home was home after all, so they wandered back to the calf pen doors expecting to be let in. They knew Bob, having been fed by him nearly all their young lives, and bawled at him when we tried to turn them to the yard gate "Git im theese darn varmits," he yelled, but they only rusnea at the gate in a heap and then dashed back and raced about again.

Boss poked his head around the corner and seeing the pandemonium, said he'd get Missus to stand in the road and he'd come and help us. This was better. When they quietened down again we guided them slowly around the yard and with three of us they had little chance to break away. Gingerly the first one looked ready to turn back, but the others were close behind so it had no option but to go. Once in the road the others quickly followed. Pausing a second they looked wildly at Missus and they were off. Boss shouted to Bob to go back through the yard and buildings and stand in the farm entrance. This was the first place to guard. I was to try and get in front of them. My attempts to do this only made them charge on faster until we passed the farm and there were grass verges alongside the road. Then they stopped for a bite. While they were absorbed in this new pastime, I managed to quietly sidle past. Ahead were open garden gates. I quickly closed them but trouble was not far away.

A drive to a house had no gate so I plonked myself in the entrance. How could I know that just around the corner was a lane. Having only strolled around one Sunday I hadn't recognised the layout. In any case I couldn't be in two places at once. Boss and Bob were having their work cut out to shift the calves. Grass was good stuff and they were quite content to nibble their way at their own speed. Annoyed at being moved on, they came running past me and out of sight. "Drat thum divals," said Bob as we rounded the corner. They'd gone down the lane. Luckily there was somebody's old abandoned van in the lane and some were walking around and poking their heads in it, while others rooted in the hedges. Boss decided to cut across a nearby field and into the lane's other entrance hoping to head them back before they tired of exploring around the van and pushed on past it. It would be touch and go whether he could make it. However, all went well and he managed to bring them up the lane. It wasn't far to the field from there and we were able to get them through the gateway without further incident. They tore around snorting in high glee, then slowed up to munch the grass.

"We'll come back and shut them in directly," said Boss. "I don't expect it will be easy once they've been out."

So it proved to be. They scattered in all directions when we tried to get them into the yard. Bob went back to get a bucket with some calf nuts in it. He walked slowly rattling it and calling "coom coom". On hearing this they pricked up their ears and a few started to follow him. They knew the sound of buckets brought food. Others, however, were reluctant to move so we had to round them up. Eventually all were shut in.

It was easier to move the smaller calves as they went into a little field called the rick barton, where there was a lean-to shed one side and several straw ricks fenced off the other. It was the other side of the farmyard. We only had to get them out of the gate, turn them into the yard and out through another gate the other end. Even so, once in the yard they went exploring, poking their noses through the bars behind which were the cow stalls, kicking around the dung heaps and not a bit inclined to go through the open gate to the field. So once more Bob collected a bucket and lured them over, while we closed in behind, and in they went, revelling in the fresh grass and their freedom.

If I'd thought this was a hectic do, the best, or rather worst, was yet to come. A few days later, Boss said to me at breakfast, "Today you can help George and Fred move the heifers." I decided not to ask what and where the heifers were until Margaret, who was doing dairy and clean out that week, and I were outside. Missus was apt to look scornful at my ignorance, but Meg, as Margaret was called, seemed to know these things. She'd been around farms before, getting feed for her horse.

As it happened George and Fred turned up immediately, so I didn't get a chance to ask her. "Ast thee's got a bite?" said Fred. I must have looked bewildered. George explained we would be gone most of the day and I'd better ask Missus for some lunch. So having collected a packet of sandwiches and a bottle of cold tea from the house, we started off. "We'm gitting thim midens ut the topun," said Fred. I could fathom out some of the things Fred said now, so I started thinking maybe I wouldn't have to ask anything about heifers.

It was a lovely morning and I began to enjoy the walk. Even so, it seemed a long way to the 'topun'. It turned out to be 'about a mile' according to George and was a long narrow field, the furthest from the farm and along the side of the main road. The 'midens' were last year's youngest calves, George informed me (presumably female and called heifers). We were to walk them about five miles to some rented fields beyond the next two villages and bring back

46

last year's older calves which were also heifers and had wintered out there. Up until now it hadn't occurred to me to think about the sex of the calves we'd moved. Of course they'd all be female if they were going to be cows but even I could see that all the cows wouldn't have had female calves. I said I hoped there weren't a lot of young bulls somewhere to be moved. George and Fred hooted with laughter, but relented and told me that the bull calves were sold soon after birth, although sometimes a particularly good one would be kept and reared.

It was no easy task to get the heifers out of the field but at last George managed to round them up.

Fred, being the eldest of us, decided he couldn't run and waited outside the gate to shoo them along the road. Being a main road there was traffic to contend with and Fred stood in the middle of the road with his hand up. I thought he just fancied himself as a cop while a queue of angry motorists were hooting their horns and shouting abuse at him. As the animals turned into the road they didn't need any encouragement. They took one look at Fred and belted in the right direction. So far so good, but George and I were supposed to get in front of them and take turns to block any openings, each going on ahead after they'd passed by. At this stage we could only keep them into the side of the road so that the cars could pass. Not far on but unknown to us, on that side was a lane and down it they all went. Now it was a case of cutting across a field and heading them off as we'd done with the younger ones a few days before. They weren't in any hurry. There was exciting stuff to find and eat in the hedge. We turned them around and George slipped back across the field while I brought them up at the rear.

Fred was still in the road where another lot of cars had collected. However, we'd had enough trouble and made them pass by singly so that George could keep ahead. Fred and I had to control the heifers as best we could. They didn't like the traffic and bellowed to say so. One man looked out of his car window to say something but hastily withdrew when a curious tongue decided to lick his face. Others shook their fists when some of the frightened animals decorated their cars with muck. It served them right for blowing their horns at them. There wasn't that amount of traffic owing to petrol restrictions and after this we had a relatively quiet time. I was glad as my feet were beginning to play me up. I was wearing my heavy shoes and was still not used to them. It seemed already hours since we'd started out, but on arrival at the first village the church clock said it was only 10.30 am. At least two more hours and four miles before lunch.

Then things really began to happen. There were some openings and drives without any gates, so that we just couldn't cope, although George took one side of the road and I the other. There were also people about and the heifers would stop and stare. Then some would go on and others didn't. Suddenly, while we were trying to keep them together and on the move, one lot disappeared. I didn't see them go. It seemed they had crept around a hedge, found an open gate, gone through a front door of a house and out of the back. A woman was hanging out her washing, she screamed and came racing out to us babbling about all this and berating us no end. On going to get them back we found them chewing her undies! There was no way out of the back garden, so we had to get them through the house again, making no end of a mess. We didn't dare laugh. It would have been too awful, but once clear we couldn't keep it in and we split our sides. We had to leave our address but I don't remember hearing any more about it later.

Meanwhile the rest were well on their way and I had to get in front of them somehow. Luckily they had kept straight on and out of the village, so I went over a hedge and along a field, coming out of a gate before they got there. A few more chasings out of an odd drive or so in the next village and then we were turning off the main road. Traffic there had been a bit of a problem although there was plenty of space, but now we were in a narrow lane and it was to be even worse.

Suddenly around a corner came a tractor with a load of hay behind. We all stopped dead. What to do? There was nowhere to pull in. Some of the heifers made up their own minds. Hay was hay wherever it was. They pushed past me and the tractor and started pulling it out from the sides of the load. At this the driver got off. "Don 'ee let thim beasts eat thic 'ay," he shouted angrily. Fred looked bewildered but George yelled at me.

"Shift 'em on and we'll let a few by at a time."

Easier said than done. They were not going to move without a struggle. I did my best but George had to come and shift them, leaving the rest with Fred. He couldn't keep them still and they all came on then, pushing to get to the hay and breaking the hedges at the sides. Some of the hay fell off the back which was lucky in a way — some of them made a beeline for it, preventing too much crush. Not that the tractor driver was very pleased. He was furious and demanded that one of us went with him to explain to his boss. Neither of us could, of course. We had too much trouble already in attempting to finish taking the animals to their new home. We went on, leaving him to it.

At last we were able to shut them into the field where they were to stay. They galloped around like mad exploring everywhere. It was past lunchtime. Thankfully we sat by the gate and ate our sandwiches and drank our cold tea, no milk or sugar, but it was like nectar from the gods. There was still the return journey with older animals from the next field. Already they were peering over the hedge at us and the

c

newcomers.

Going back was not as hair raising. These heifers had been used to being moved and apart from a chase over a field, when they pushed through a gap we hadn't noticed, all went well. We put them in a field near the farm. " 'Twill be best for them bulim midens," said Fred. I hadn't any idea of what he meant, but was too tired to bother. It was five o'clock and I could hear them still in the milking sheds. Wearily I staggered into the house. I went upstairs for a rest before tea. My feet were sore, my legs and head ached. Still, it had been an adventure and fun I thought, and I fell asleep.

Chapter Six

WHEN IGNORANCE IS NOT BLISS

It was about this time that I began to discover the facts of life (cow-wise).

One day during afternoon milking boss said we would keep one of the cows in as she was due to calve and had had a difficult time at the previous calving. I had no idea of any of it and had hoped it would all happen without me knowing.

Being springtime some cows had calved out in the field. They just came in to a stall to suckle the calf on their own for a few days and then the calf was weaned. After this they both bawled a lot for a while and then things went back to normal.

The same evening Margaret and I had been out for a cycle ride and gone to bed. Suddenly there was a loud knocking on our door. Missus shouted, "Come on you girls, Boss needs help in the cowshed." We hastily dressed and made our way there. I was feeling sick with apprehension. Margaret seemed quite unconcerned. Nothing seemed to bother her.

We went in the shed. Boss was tying a rope on to the calves feet, just protruding from the rear of the cow. He indicated we were to pull the rope when he gave the signal and to loose it in between. Apparently, as the cow strained to expel the calf we were to help her on. It was obviously a big one and going to be difficult. We didn't seem to be getting anywhere and then after a hefty pull the rope broke. Boss went to get another stronger one. I felt sorry for the cow. It all seemed such a nasty business.

Subsequently I got used to it, but this first time I was suffering with her. Not that she was really suffering, just tired and fed up, and after a few more tries she decided to lie down. This made it more difficult for us, but surprisingly the next few contractions brought the calf away and we fell over with the sudden loosening of the rope. Needless to say it had to be in a heap of muck.

Boss picked up the calf and held it upside down, shaking it and poking its nose with a bit of straw. He said this was to expel any mucus and get it breathing well. It had been a long time being born and was not very lively. The cow then expelled the afterbirth. At the time I didn't know what this was. I only found out later from Margaret. The cow then began licking the calf and mooing to it, as pleased as punch. They both were now all right. Boss said he'd stay to see the calf started suckling and we could go back to bed.

I pondered on how we had helped a cow to have a live calf and that it all seemed worthwhile after all. Also I had had quite an experience and I was no longer so ignorant, or so I thought.

However, this was not the end of it. A few days later I was tying up the cows for milking, quite often doing one stall on my own now, while the men were in the bigger shed doing likewise. I noted one cow had a discharge. Now, I thought, was the time to show them. They would realise I was no longer a learner and was quite equal to them. I hurried over to the other shed and went up to George explaining that there was a cow in my lot and it was going to calve. Would he come over to see. He looked at me strangely but said he would. He was younger than the other chaps and single. Spare our blushes for what happened next. He took me to look at the cow and went a deep red. I realised something was wrong and said: "What's the matter, isn't she going to calve?"

George hummed and hawed and didn't look at me. Then said, "No she's not. Look, cows be like wimmin, you'll 'ave to sort it out for yerself." With which he beat a hasty retreat.

I felt more of a fool than ever and decided never to say anything again, but to find out details from Margaret. She seemed to know most of it. So much for my self-esteem. For several days I avoided George if I could, until it seemed to be forgotten.

I gleaned some of the facts from Margaret, but not all as I found out during the next episode in my education. Looking back it was more funny than embarrassing, although it was that as well.

After breakfast one day Boss told me to go with Fred and bring some heifers into the yard from the ones we had recently brought back to the farm. After my previous gaff, I decided not to ask anything but went along with Fred. He opened the gate of the yard around which were the bulls' and calf pens. Then we went out to the field where the heifers were kept. I stood one side of the gate to head them to the farm. Fred opened it and went in to get them out.

"Us'll 'ave tu git thic bullin un ut," he said. "Don 'ee 'ave 'um all ut."

I couldn't make much of this, so waited to see what happened. A few of them were jumping about on each other and these Fred tried to drive to the gate. They seemed willing enough but the rest decided to come as well. He shouted at me to let the first ones out and then stop the rest. I did my best but a couple of them slipped past me. We ended up with about half of them and managed to leave the rest milling round the gate in the field. Fred shrugged, " 'T'ule 'ave tu du," he said as we guided them down to the farm and into the yard. Boss was there and told me to go back into the cowstall. There was a small one here where the cows with calves were usually tied up. Bob was cleaning it out.

" 'Ers 'aving thic bull ut," said Bob. "Thic un's nasty."

At this point we could see over the stall wall that Boss had opened the bull's pen door and gone in to untie him. Bob shuddered, " 'Ers nasty," he said again. As he spoke out rushed the bull and tore around the yard roaring and tossing up some galvanised sheets around the water trough. The heifers bunched in the corner, looking interested and unafraid. Boss and Fred came into the stall and said it was best to leave them to get on with it. The bull would serve the right one.

As the light began to dawn on me, I wondered how I could have been so naive. I looked round and wondered where Bob had disappeared to. Boss laughed, "Look up there," he said, and there was Bob sitting on a beam shaking with fright. When Boss had opened the door to come in he thought the bull might come in as well and had climbed up. Being small and wizened he looked just like a monkey!

Boss was keeping an eye on things outside and when he wasn't looking I had a peep so as I'd know just what went on. Soon Fred and he went out to get the bull back in the pen. He had quietened down now and followed Boss, who was rattling some cow cake in a bucket he'd taken out with him, into the pen. Fred helped to tie him up.

Bob came down off his perch looking rather sheepish. He sucked his pipe, and pushing back his cap scratched his head. "Wull us niver knows. Bes be 'ut the way sno' mide," he excused himself.

Fred called me to help take the heifers back to the field.

I walked out nonchalantly as if it was just another item in a morning's work. Inside I was thinking that there couldn't be much else to discover. However, later on I learnt that sometimes 'thim bullin midens', as Fred called them, had to be brought in more than once to see their friend the bull as they hadn't 'held'. Then there was an odd one which would never have a calf and was called a freemartin. It would be one of a twin, the other being a bull calf.

The bulls were never allowed in the field so the cows also had to be 'sid to' as Bob said. Usually Boss led the older bull out in the yard for the cows by a pole attached to his nose ring. He was fairly quiet and they were old hands, so it didn't take long. Usually this happened when we had turned them into the yards after milking, ready to go out to the fields.

At milking time I could now get on with stripping and hand milking a few cows whose teats were too long for the cups of the milking machine. Also some of the older ones would just refuse to give down any more milk on it. I had become used to their funny ways and knew which had to be watched for fidgeting or kicking.

A few weeks before calving the cows were dried off. This was to give them a rest before they had another calf. Usually others came in to take their place. The heifers having had their first calf would sometimes be very difficult. Some had very small teats on a tight udder and the cups of the machine would fall off. Then one had to stand and hold them on. This would rectify itself as the milk decreased. Also, not being used to any form of milking, some of the heifers would kick and jump around so that one had to hold its nose, while a rope was tied round to keep the hind legs together. Most settled down after a few days, but we had a couple of 'thim beddy beggers', as Bob called them. We always had to tie them.

55

Boss wanted me to take over using the machines in our shed, so that he or Fred wouldn't always have to come in when haymaking started. Bob couldn't cope with 'thim danged thins'. It meant taking each off at the right time and keeping three going. He also had his pipe to see to, although not allowed by Boss if he was there during milking. He stuck it in his pocket, having a draw in between, when no one was looking. It was a wonder he never caught himself alight.

Boss stayed around watching while I was learning to handle the milking buckets, plug in the pipe and put the teat cups on the cows. There was a glass section in the tube which took the milk so that one could see when it finished coming. I soon got the hang of it and felt terribly clever, but pride comes before a fall. At this stage I was not left to do it on my own. Boss and I took turn about.

One day a fresh heifer was brought in, dainty and long legged but with exceptionally small teats and tight udder. She was very frisky and it took two of us to get the machine on and off her, after tying her legs. Boss said she was all right to strip. She couldn't kick with the rope on. I gingerly sat down with a bucket, putting my shoulder under her hind leg. One touch and there I was, out in the gutter, legs in the air, and covered in the muck I'd slithered in. The bucket rattled off down the shed. Boss, who'd gone out to the dairy, came back to see what was going on. He helped me up. I was very shaken and had a big lump on my elbow. "No she hadn't kicked," I told him, "she jumped." She was looking round at us enough to say 'That'll show you'.

"We'd better leave her," said Boss, she'll calm down in a while and you'd best go and get cleaned up — I'll finish off."

Meanwhile the war was going on and older age groups had to go into the services. Jack the carter was called up in the army. Boss applied for another land girl and Freda arrived. She was cockney and no end of a wit. There were now three of us. Margaret and I were dairy maids and spent spare time on the land. Freda took over Jack's job with the horses and also learnt to drive the tractors. She fitted in as if she'd been doing it all her life. Well built, she confessed to a few muscle pains, but didn't seem to suffer like I had. She had helped in her father's fruit shop before and was used to lifting boxes. Also she didn't have to learn to milk which tried one's wrists and fingers.

Margaret and I had alternate weekends off but Freda was able to go off every weekend. She usually went to London to see her parents. She came back to tell us there had been some raids but they hadn't thought it bad enough to go into the shelters. A few streets were bombed to the ground and fires from incendiary bombs had destroyed others. We began to appreciate our life in the country. Although the hours were long and the work was hard, we were largely unaffected by the war. The siren would go occasionally as enemy planes flew over, but their targets were the railways and cities. One was shot down not far away and the German pilot parachuted out. On landing he was quickly marched off by the locals.

Freda thought life rather quiet after London and decided to liven things up a bit. Margaret and I had been to the pictures a few times but we were normally too tired after work to do very much. Our day began at six and finished at six, whereas Freda's hours were from seven to five. We all understood, however, that when hay and corn harvest came we would be expected to work until dark at times.

Freda found out that there were dances up at the nearby camp. We decided to go along with her. It was the first time we had dressed in civvies for some time. Usually we would put on a clean Land Army shirt and breeches with the green pullover, kept for going out. We didn't need them for working. We wore dungarees and a matching jacket then. So it was quite an occasion as we dolled ourselves up and got on our bikes to go.

On arriving we found the place packed out with soldiers and girls; some from the attached ATS and some civilians. I'd never been to a dance before as I was not allowed to go at home and had no idea of how to dance. Freda and Margaret soon were asked by two soldiers and went off. I was feeling very left out of it, when a young chap did come and ask me at last. He, however, seemed as gormless as me, and after we'd trod on each other's toes a few times, bumped into some other couples, who gave us a filthy look, and the music stopped, he disappeared. I was left with sore feet from his heavy boots and felt fed up.

Freda and Margaret seemed to be partnered for the evening, so I decided to go home. Not wanting to admit the truth, I found them and said I didn't feel well. They were willing to come back with me but I said I'd be all right.

After that they often went to the camp dances, but I made excuses and never went again. It wasn't my cup of tea at all.

Chapter Seven

HAY NONNY NO

A lot of the field work was done by Boss and Fred, and now Freda instead of Jack. However, Margaret and I did our share on our alternate weeks out of the cowsheds. So it happened one day that while Fred and Freda were drilling kale and mangold seed with the tractor, Boss took me to help under-sow the spring corn with grass seed. This was a part of the rotation of crops. In those days grass sowing was done with a contraption like a wheelbarrow, but instead of the barrow there was a long seed box. My job was to guide in front, pulling a rope, while Boss wheeled behind and the seed dispersed as we went along. Then at intervals we refilled the seed box from a sack. Forward and back, forward and back, we crossed and recrossed the field. It was a warm day and although I was more used to work by now, my legs began to ache and my hands became sore with the rope. Then, after a break for a drink which we had brought, we went on again.

When we went back to the farm for dinner, there was just over half the field done. Afternoon saw us once more on the job. By now I was feeling not unlike a horse, but without power. It was a great relief to finish at about 4 pm and go in to help milking.

Another day was spent leading the horse while Boss walked behind earthing up the potatoes.

By now the days had lengthened, the wireless predicted a fine spell and Boss brought out the mowing machine to cut the grass for hay. First, however, the long knives had to be sharpened and taken to be mended at the agricultural machinery depot. A spare one must be handy in case of damage on a stone, though earlier we had collected most of them. I remembered how I had hated the job, but could now see the necessity of it.

The first field to cut was one undersown the previous year. It was clover and mixed grass and according to Boss would take a long time to dry. The weather was hot and the sun shone all day until late at night. The best time was early morning. As I went along the lane to fetch the cows, the birds were singing in the fresh air. One felt good to be alive.

It was my week out and after breakfast I had to go away to the fields. There we were having to hand hoe mangolds just coming up. I had a job to keep up with George. He sliced away at the weeds effortlessly, while I was scraping about like an old hen. However, after a while, I began to get the hang of it, but bent at an angle my back started to ache and the hoe renewed the sore places on my hands. It seemed each new job affected different bits of me. How long before I would become totally used to it all? I said as much to George.

"Oh, we all get a bit stiff with fresh jobs," he said.

I thought in my case this was an understatement. He wasn't one to say much although I could understand him better than Bob or Fred. He waited for me as we finished the lines and we had a stretch before starting down the next ones. Looking at the whole piece, it seemed a daunting task. Although I had changed to an Aertex shirt I still had to wear dungarees. Girls didn't go about in shorts then and clothes were rationed in any case, so we had to rely on our uniform: with thick socks and heavy shoes the heat was very tiring.

"Well we'll be here a few weeks," said George. "We have to thin them out after."

Well I wouldn't — I would be in the cowsheds this time next week and Margaret would be out here. That would be a change, even if I had to come back to it the week after. For the first time I envied Freda sitting on the horse rake, tossing around the grass in the hayfield. But then I'd be no good at that, I was still scared of horses, although I'd led them on hoeing jobs — but to be in charge of one! It was also decidedly bumpy and one needed a good padding! Being slim, no doubt my bones would have had a good rattling. Occasionally I had to ride my bike down to the agricultural depot with a mowing knife wrapped in a sack to be sharpened. Looking back it was really a silly thing to do with it balanced across the handlebars. There was no one else to spare to go and such was the haste to make hay while the sun shone, that it wasn't considered. There was not much traffic about and I was glad to get away for a break, having a nice little rest while the knife was sharpened. Cycling back in the warm sunshine was better than back aching hoeing. The ground had become very hard in the dry weather and it was like scraping the road.

The weather kept fine and a few days later Boss said we would go haymaking in the afternoon. Everyone went up to the field except Bob. He never did any field work. When he'd finished with the yard he would go in the garden or do other odd jobs. Boss told us which job we would each do. He would make the hayrick with help from Margaret. George and I were to pitch the hay into the elevator which would drop it down to the rick. Fred would sweep it in with the tractor and Freda would go on rowing it up.

So we started. It was jolly hard work digging out picks of

hay from the massive loads Fred brought. If it came sideways it was easier but any brought head on rolled itself round and round and refused to budge. After a while George called Fred to halt while we cleared some of it and Fred stopped to give us a hand.

I'd worn my Land Army hat, although it was felt, to keep off the sun. By now it was sticking to my head and I was soaked with sweat. Was I relieved when Boss said, "George and Ellen had better go in to milk." Fred and the others would carry on.

I remembered George's words from early days about being glad to go in milking in hay time. However, it would be my first time in charge of our cowshed and I was a bit nervous. Bob had brought in the cows and we three tied them up. George started up the engine and went off to milk his lot and I carried in the buckets to get on with ours. Bob was going to milk the odd ones and we would do the stripping in between. Then while I finished off he would go and give George a hand. It all took longer than normal with two less people but it was finished at last. I suddenly felt that I had passed a milestone. There would still be a lot of new experiences and I was yet far from a proficient farm worker, but I could cope with milking cows on and off the machine and to me it was success. I even felt amiable towards the wicked looking Katy and patted her when I untied her. She, however, tossed her head as usual and wasn't a bit impressed. After tea it was back to the field.

The weather continued fine and Boss or Fred went on cutting grass. Each day continued the same: milking, hoeing mangolds or kale until lunch, then haymaking and milking, and after tea haymaking again until dark. In the hayfield, if Freda wasn't raking she would pitch hay in the elevator and I would go onto the rick to help. Then my feet would sink and fall about in the soft hay, while I struggled to pass it back to Margaret and Boss. I always seemed to tread on the bit I was trying to move or a big wad would fall from the elevator on my head and knock my hat sideways. One day it got pulled off and went merrily round with the hay on the elevator until someone snatched it off at the bottom. We all laughed but Boss said to be careful not to get too near again. I could have been hurt.

Sometimes we'd get a break when the hay was coming in from the furthest parts of the field. Then we'd have a swig of cold tea — no milk or sugar. To us, sweating and thirsty, it tasted like nectar from the gods and it was thirst quenching, but a drop was enough for me or I found I would feel sick in the heat. Although there was so much more to do, I looked forward to milking times. My face and arms had a chance to cool off. They had burnt, peeled off, and burnt again, especially my nose. Suntan creams were not around then and the only relief was calamine lotion. Although a great balm, one could only dab it on. It didn't stay on my red nose very well and I ended up with white patches, rather like a clown. Being painful to wash I put on more, then looking as if my face had been in the flour bag. I wore dungarees and socks: although hot, at least they kept my legs from burning. I think I suffered more than the other girls as they had darker skins and my complexion at that time was very fair. Years ahead my face would still burn, but my arms below the elbow became weathered from always having sleeves rolled up, except in the very cold.

After we finished making hay of the first year leys and had built numerous ricks, it was time to start on the meadow grass. This had been laid up for a couple of months after the cows had grazed it. It also took a long time to dry as the fields were low lying. These being quite a distance away and not very accessible, the hay was to be brought back to the farm on wagons. It was easier to cart it in the summer and came in useful for the calves in the sheds in winter. It took a lot longer. After the hay was rowed it had to be pitched onto the wagons. There were three in the field and the two horses and one tractor with which it was hoped to make a shuttle run. Freda would row up the hay while Boss and Fred loaded leaving George, Margaret and me to pitch the hay up. As soon as one wagon was full, Boss and Freda, having finished rowing, would take it back with the tractor to the rick yard, unload it and bring the tractor back empty. Meanwhile we went on loading the other wagons. It seemed to work quite well, as we were slower with one pair of hands less and, in any case, unloading is quicker.

The horses seemed to move on at a 'getup' and 'whoaah', and amused themselves with mouthfuls of hay between. The only bother was in re-tethering the wagons when changing over. They didn't want to be disturbed from their munching and snorted their disapproval.

The weather still kept fine. It really was a flaming June that year. There was no hold-up in the haymaking and soon all was done. Eventually it rained and there was the fresh smell of earth and poignant farmyard as the dust was laid. Boss heaved a sigh of relief. Grass was now getting short and rain was badly needed to bring on the aftermath to feed the cows and young stock. The corn now in ear needed rain to swell the grain. All the roots were suffering from the drought.

The hayricks had temporarily been covered with canvas sheets. They were going to be thatched by an old chap called 'Shep'. He had once been a shepherd, but now only did all the thatching and a few odd jobs. I had to first help him make the thatch. It consisted of me pulling out straw along the side of one of the previous years wheat straw ricks. No easy task this. One needed long sleeves not to get scratched and cut — still my hands suffered. Shep would then lay it out, some one way and some the other, until he had a bundle which he bound with more straws. This was a skilled job. It had to be made properly to keep out the wet.

In contrast to the other men, Shep wore an old black trilby hat. He had a long droopy moustache which was a gingery colour. He didn't have a pipe like Bob but every now and again he'd take out a tin from his waistcoat pocket and from it poke something up his nose. I was fascinated and when he offered me some to try I took it. The next minute I was sneezing my head off and felt as if a pepperpot had been emptied in my nose. Shep only laughed while my eyes watered as well.

" 'Tis snuff and 'twill clear yer ed," he said.

I didn't want my head cleared, anyway not like that. I'd heard of snuff but had no idea of its use until now, nor had I met anyone who took it. No wonder his moustache was ginger. It didn't make him sneeze, but I could see his eyes were a bit watery behind his silver rimmed spectacles. When I recovered a bit I asked him why. It seemed he'd been taking it for a long time and was used to it. Well it was my first and I vowed, last time, as once more we got going on the thatch making.

After working all hours haymaking it seemed peculiar to go back to having evenings free. We brought out our bikes and went exploring the countryside or went with Margaret to her home, where we'd have supper and then cycle back in the dusk. As we approached the farm the smell of the hay in the ricks at this time was particularly sweet. One felt great satisfaction after all the labour.

Chapter Eight

DOUBLE TROUBLE

Somewhere around this time the powers that be decided it would be a good idea to put the clocks forward another hour. It would help the war effort no end! Munitions factories working in shifts could arrange them better and farmers could go on working longer hours in the light. There was no thought for the animals. It had been bad enough in the spring when the clocks had been put forward one hour. Cows that had been used to milking at regular times didn't want to come in at 5 am instead of 6 and the milk yield would be down. Similarly in the afternoon. It took weeks for them to adjust and production was lost in the process.

Now it was going to happen all over again. Boss was dead against it. No matter what they said or other people did, we were going to carry on work at the usual time and he would not be putting our clocks forward. His cows weren't going to be messed about again!

At first none of us girls minded. It seemed clever to be different. The farm work went on as usual. However, trouble began quite quickly. Mrs Bob and Mrs Fred complained at having to get meals earlier for the men than the children. "Moi missus dun like un," said Fred. "Thic bus be gon tu, so 'er can't git to thic shops." They both moaned about it to me, hoping I would tell Boss but, knowing him, I didn't bother or take much notice. However, when I was going home on the weekend and went to catch the bus myself — it didn't turn up. It was only a five minute walk to the main road and bus stop from the farm, so I went back there. Missus was surprised to see me. Didn't I know the bus times she asked, when I explained. She and Boss always went by car. I knew there was one at two o'clock and they only went every two hours and finished at eight, now that they had been cut to save petrol. Then it dawned. Of course, it was three o'clock really and the next one would be four o'clock. There wouldn't be much of the afternoon left by the time I arrived home. Catching the last bus back would also mean I'd be back earlier too. Being an hour behind everyone else was not going to be so funny. I began to feel sorry for Bob and Fred knowing they were getting nagged about it at home.

Soon after this we girls decided to go to the pictures. We hadn't been for a long time. We cycled into town and parked our bikes at Margaret's house and walked to the cinema. The big film we'd especially wanted to see was half over and looking at the cinema clock we realised why. It was maddening! We couldn't get into town any earlier after leaving work, so it was going to be the same any week. We might as well give up going.

Other instances occurred and we were constantly reckoning the time as against other people. I did mention about these things to Boss but it didn't effect him and he ignored it. So we resigned ourselves until the autumn, when other people would put their clocks back and we would once again be normal.

After the thatching I was helping George with cutting and making the hedges. He cut the top and sides with a hook. Then I had to clear up the small spindly bits and he would deftly weave in the longer pieces, making the bottom of the hedge thick again. When we had a big heap of bits he'd make a bonfire. It was hot work. I had to wear wellingtons against the prickly hedgings and as they were dry they made a good blaze.

One day Boss said we girls could have a week's holiday in turn if we liked, before the harvest began. Or be paid an extra week's wages. It seemed that none of the men ever had any time off. Maybe they preferred the money. Fred certainly had several children to keep. He never seemed to go anywhere except to have a 'point' at the local, Saturday nights, so I heard. I suppose Bob's baccy cost a bit and Fred had a rolled fag sometimes when Boss was out of the way. The wages were not much then and they all had gardens and grew most of their vegetables. They were used to work and probably wouldn't have known what to do with a holiday. In war time also there was little or no means to go anywhere.

For myself, I was glad to go home for a week back to normal time and to have a really long rest. I just mooched about noticing things in the countryside I hadn't done before. I looked critically at the nearby farms. Some hadn't finished their hay! Their cows udders didn't look full! And what a patchy lot of roots! I realised I was working on a very efficient farm and I had been a part in making it so. That and the change bucked me up no end and it was with renewed energy I went back at the end of the week. Just as well — Margaret and Freda were having their week off so I had to help Fred take the horse and hoe up to the root field. We hadn't been there since early in the haymaking, when we had singled out the mangolds. Now the whole lot was plastered with weeds.

"Gor dang us," said Fred. "Be a prupper miss."

I'd done a similar job before with Jack planting the potatoes, so I knew I had to lead the horse up and down the rows while Fred guided the hoe. At least the ground was soft and the blade swiftly cut a passage up through first the potatoes then the mangolds. These had grown and were like small oranges with a leafy top above the ground. When we'd finished we could see the rows again, the weeds were all chopped up in between.

" 'Ope 'twill be foin," said Fred, "ur them beggars wull grow s'now."

I looked at him doubtfully, not understanding.

"Oh arrh, these u'll see," he said.

He didn't explain, so I decided not to ask what he meant, but wait and see.

After this it rained for a few days. George and I were tidying up the barn and sorting out sacks for the corn later on. Those with holes in were put on one side for mending. One was cut up for patches which we sewed on with a sacking needle and thread. At least it was better than getting wet outside.

As soon as the weather cleared Boss said we'd better go up and see what we could do in the roots. They were in a worse mess than before. I could see what Fred had meant now. The weeds had just grown back in. Boss decided hand hoeing would be best. Then we'd heap up the weeds and take them to the end of the rows to burn later. It was a mucky job. The mud stuck to our hoes and our boots in lumps with the weeds. It was difficult not to tread them in again. It looked like being a long job. We cleared a small patch and made our way back to milking. Fred was grinning at me — I laughed as well, waiting for some comment. "Oh arrh, thee's 'ull laf — asn't sin thees mug yit." I guessed it must be muddy. As I went into the farm to get my milking apron I glanced in the mirror in the back passage. Sure enough I had streaked mud round my nose. One picked up bad habits while working with the men. They usually wiped their noses with the back of their hands and I often found myself doing the same.

Messing with the weeds I'd made my hands pretty dirty and rubbed it on my face. It crossed my mind that people paid to have mud packs in beauty salons, so it might improve my complexion. Probably not this earthy sort though!

The days passed and we slowly got the roots clean again. The weather had now cleared and it became easier as the weeds shrivelled up when cut off. We were able to make little bonfires of them near the hedge, keeping a sharp eye on them not to spread. By now the potatoes had a good green hulm on them, so when the whole field was completely cleared of weeds I was once more leading the horse up and down the rows of potatoes. This time Fred was guiding the 'earther' behind. It pushed the earth up each side round the plants leaving a trench in the middle. When we finished they looked like rows of little soldiers all neat and tidy.

" 'T'will keep 'un prupper," said Fred.

He and Bob never explained what they meant, assuming I knew or ought to know all about it. *They did!* If I asked they thought it funny and would grin. If they tried to explain, I had a job to understand their language and was none the wiser. Sometimes I asked George as he wasn't as broadly spoken, but usually Boss told me what I wanted to know. I asked him about the potatoes. It seems that as roots grow they tend to surface and rain would also wash the earth away. It didn't matter with mangolds or swedes and turnips but potatoes had to be kept in the earth or they would get green and hard. Also by earthing them up it would be easier to lift them without damage later on.

The days became sultry and I seemed to itch a lot, especially around my middle. Then I noticed a red rash. I thought it might be the heat, as it soon spread all over me. Missus said I should go to the doctor as it might be catching. It seemed a bit silly as I didn't feel ill or anything, but I thought I'd better go. His verdict was that it was caused by dirt. He thought I'd probably picked it up on a bus or public place from someone. It was very contagious and horrors! — I must bath in a solution of Jeyes Fluid frequently. Also wash all my cloths in it.

I felt like a leper, and what would I smell like? Margaret and Freda thought it a great joke and gave me a wide berth. For myself, my skin was so irritated I thought I'd better get on with it. The bathing made it sting but with plenty of highly scented soap, although it was a peculiar mixture, at least I didn't smell like the public lavatories. I also used the soap on my clothes but then hung them out in the air which diluted the overall perfume. After a few days there was a distinct improvement and gradually the rash went.

I had been feeling very irritable what with the itching and the nightly job of clothes washing. So I wasn't amused when one day George said that we'd soon be harvesting and probably we girls would get bitten up with the bugs. I thought he was having me on and decided to take no notice. Then I remembered his gloomy talk before the haymaking. He'd been right that that was very hard, hot work compared to milking cows. But bugs! Only dirty people had bugs didn't they? Already I'd just had one rash from an unknown source. Well there was no point in worrying about it till the time came.

I think George resented women about the place and delighted in trying to make everything seem as hard or nasty as possible, especially to me, as I was smaller than the other girls. I noticed too that he'd been rather sarky since I had taken over milking on my own in the haymaking days. I would have to again when we started harvest or Boss was particularly busy. I expect he wanted to put me in my place. Not many men liked girls doing their job as well as them in those days, even though it was essential to the war effort.

Chapter Nine

HARVEST MOON

It was time at last to cut the corn. Boss and Fred got out the binder and drove to the oatfield which had been planted the previous autumn. This corn was called 'winter oats' and was now tall and a pale gold. I was told to come as well with George. He had to go around the outside of the field with a rip-hook and cut swathes of corn to make a path for the tractor and binder. I was to gather the stalks up in bundles and tie them up. George was pleased he could show me how to twist a few around a bundle and tuck in the ends to neaten. Then I had to lean them in the hedge.

It was a long way all round the field, and after Boss and Fred had the binder ready they joined us and set to work clearing around the opposite way. It took most of the morning, but at last they decided there was enough space to start the main work, while George and I went on to finish round the edge. Boss drove the tractor slowly along the path we had cut and Fred sat on the binder to watch as the corn was cut and bound into sheaves, which dropped off the binder.

It was no smooth passage to produce the sheaves. The corn might get tangled and not bind or drop out properly, or the string might break. Then Fred would yell to Boss to stop and they would have to see to whatever the trouble was. It was soon dinner-time and we went back to the farm.

In the afternoons we were joined by the other girls. Our job now was to 'hyle' up the sheaves. I never discovered how this word was spelt. It might have been 'aisle'. I think it must have been a very local word as it wasn't used anywhere else that I know of. Fred called it 'ailing 'em oop'. Anyway, we 'ailed em oop'. This meant picking up one sheaf under each arm and ramming the corn heads together, while firmly pushing the stalk ends on to the ground. Then two more sheaves close to these and a further two next, making six in all, put together like a little ark. If it rained most of it would drain off and when it stopped, the corn would dry off again. Boss said that these oats would have to stay in the field about three weeks to dry the sap out of the stalks, so it was important to get them 'stooked' up properly. Later I found this was the expression used in other places, although I hadn't heard it then.

It seemed easy enough collecting the sheaves from the hedge and those falling from the binder, but oh how my arms began to ache and the stubble began to scratch my ankles, sticking right through my socks. I was glad I'd taken notice of Fred and worn a long sleeved shirt. "Thic carn 'ull gid 'ee summat," he warned us the day before we started. As it was my hands became red and sore all over. Bits of odd straw sticking out unexpectedly gave one a poke in the face. All in all I was relieved when it was milking time for George and me. I felt sorry for the other girls who would be carrying on until five and after. However, it looked as though we'd also be going back after tea, as they hadn't cut very much of the field yet. I'd have to take charge of one lot of milkers, it would make a break and I was quite attached to the cows by now.

After tea we went back to the field and worked till dusk.

d

Sometimes a startled rabbit would race out of the uncut corn and scoot off into the hedge. Or a partridge fly up and away. The evenings were not as long now and as we made our way back to the farm we could see the moon beginning to come up, but as yet it was only a sliver in the sky.

It took a few more days to finish the field. There had been quite a few stoppages. Owing to a few heavy storms earlier on, some of the oats had 'gone down' and these patches had to be cut by driving the tractor and binder along one way which took more time. Then we would have to look around to see if any sheaves had fallen over and put them up again.

At last it was done and then we had a change. Some of the longer hedge parings which had been cut earlier on had been bundled into faggots. We had to load a trailer and with a tractor, take them to the corn fields to make 'staddles'. The bundles were laid round and across to form big oblongs. Then we had to bring a load of loose straw to cover them. This would form bases to build the corn stacks on later. Depending on the size of the field there might be several. Between times we would go up to the oats and put up any sheaves which seemed to fall down for no reason. Maybe the rabbits played around at night and disturbed them. Most likely it was birds pecking out the ears in the early morning.

Soon after, Boss said he was going to cut the wheat. We would have to 'oil it oop' just the same but as soon as that was finished it would be carted. The straw was shorter and stiffer than the oats and didn't have much sap, so there was no need to leave it in the field very long. So that day we went up to the wheat-field and followed the same pattern as before, binding up the first swathes around the edge of the field and then hyling up the sheaves. In some ways it was worse than the oats had been. The straw was very slippery and the cut stubble like razor edges. Only the sheaves were easier to push together; being shorter and stockier they didn't give like the oats or fall over so easily.

After a few days we started the carting. Both the tractor and horses were used. Shep had come to help and he and Fred would make the loads while Boss, George, Fred and myself would pitch up the sheaves. We had to place them around the wagon and the loader would lock them in together and in the middle. It was quite a skilled job so that they didn't slide out as the load grew higher. We had to lead on the horse in between the rows. When one load was full it was taken to the rick base. Then Shep started building the rick while Boss or Fred pitched off the sheaves, one of us handing them back to Shep. After the first few loads we were able to keep the rick going at the same time as loading the wagons, by just having one pitcher for them.

It was a very pleasant day and although the sun was warm I was thinking it wasn't too bad pitching up on the load. One mustn't go too fast or Fred the loader couldn't cope. Maybe I felt a little drowsy. However, I went to lead the horse forward. It was Judy — she kicked up her heels and went at a trot. I tripped on the stubble and fell over. The lead was wrenched from my hand and I looked up in horror to see the wagon wheel just about to run over my head. Quickly I jerked away and lay shaking with fright as the horse and wagon continued on down the row. I heard Fred yelling at the horse but felt unable to move. Then George came over to stop the horse and see what had happened. He helped me up. I wasn't hurt at all, but I was overcome, I just burst into tears.

George looked dumb-struck, but Fred, having by now clambered down from the load, said, "Don ee moin mide, er be a divil ut toimes." The devil herself was quite unconcernedly munching at some grass in the stubble. I recovered and it was back to the job. Ever after that I was very careful when leading either of the horses, although Punch, the other one, was the one we had used in the roots and was much more docile.

We went on loading up the sheaves and taking the full loads back to the rick. It was growing now and the elevator had been pulled in front to carry the sheaves up on it. At the top it was roofed in to resemble a small cottage. Then the next one would be started. Later on Shep would thatch them.

Time went by with the same daily routine. Milking, corn hauling, milking and corn hauling again till late. There were now several ricks in the field.

Meanwhile we girls had been itching, around our middles mostly, but also other places, where any clothes were tight. We inspected ourselves at night and found lumpy weals. Margaret used to stand stark naked in front of the wardrobe mirror trying to see behind, while we others giggled and offered to count them for her. The harvest bugs had certainly made a good meal of her, but we also had our share. George's prophesy again. Missus advised us to dab the lumps with calamine lotion, which we did. It was very soothing, but we looked most peculiar with pink blobs in funny places. We tried not to scratch when the men were around. We knew we'd get ribbed over it. I could just hear Fred, "Thic uns du loik swate mate s'no." I supposed they were immune as they had been on the farm many years. Anyway, they didn't admit to having any trouble. George glanced at us curiously a few times as we fidgeted a bit, but we didn't let on.

Just as Boss had decided to start on another field we had a few days rain. This relieved us quite a bit, but it was short-lived. Soon after the rain stopped and the wheat dried out quickly. Then we were back to the 'oiling up' and carting, and more harvest bugs. Time passed as each day we worked until dusk. Each evening when we finished, the moon seemed to be growing bigger in the sky.

Having finished the wheat there was dredge corn to cut. This was the worst. It was a mixture of oats, barley and peas, the hulm of which made it very tangly. Boss managed some of it with the binder, but in the end had to finish with the mowing machine. This meant a lot of it was loose and we had to tie it into bundles as we had that around the edges of the field. It was horrid stuff to try and tie up into any semblance of a sheaf and having managed that, they wouldn't stick up but wobbled about in all directions. Not only that, but the bits of barley would stick in our clothes, or we'd catch a foot in an uncut bit of pea hulm and fall over. However, we struggled on and got it done. This also had to stay in the field to dry out.

Over three weeks had passed, so that the oats were now considered fit to haul. A few days later all of these were safely gathered into the ricks — the harvest was nearly over.

The evenings were almost dark when we finished. The moon was coming up full and shone a lovely golden light over the stubbled fields and rows of ricks. They represented a lot of hard work and we were proud of our efforts.

While we were waiting for the dredge corn to dry out, Boss decided to take a second crop of hay from the clover field. The grass had grown quite high since it had been cut in June and was fit to cut again. The mornings had a chill about them and there was dew on the grass, so that it was later before he could get up to cut it. Then it didn't dry quickly as it had in the early summer. Freda had to go and toss it about again and again. It was quite some time before it was anywhere near fit for hauling. We others had been picking up the dredge corn sheaves each day, which wouldn't stay put, and getting more staddles ready for the ricks.

At last the hay was ready, although we had to wait till

afternoons to pick it up and evening work was out, as the air got damper again then. It was much easier doing a bit each day and nothing like the hectic time of earlier on. It was the same when we had finished and started on the dredge corn. We had to wait till the sun was well up and had dried off the early dews.

So the harvest came to an end and autumn was on us with fresh tasks to tackle.

Chapter Ten

SEASON OF MISTS

We went back to the hedges. There were so many of them. Each year some were made and others just had to be trimmed if they had been made within a few years. Unless there were many holes where the cattle rubbed against them and pushed their noses in looking for a juicy morsel. Rabbits often made burrows which loosened the earth and a gap appeared. Some had blackberries which after the hot summer were already ripe. One evening we girls decided to go and pick some before they were cut off. It seemed a shame for them to go to waste. I had happy memories of childhood jaunts when we went on Saturdays, taking a picnic and returning scratched and tired. It was bath night and how our legs hurt in the water, but it never deterred us from going again.

This time we found a good crop in one of the meadows and were picking away when I put my hand on a wasp. It stung like mad and my hand began to swell. As we already had a few pounds of blackberries we decided to go back to the farm. Missus bathed my hand in vinegar and by now it was almost twice the size. It eased a bit. The next day it was still swollen but being the left arm I managed some milking just stripping with one hand. Old Bob had to do the rest. When I told him about it he just said, as usual, "Aw arrh, thic uns be varmits."

However, we enjoyed the fruit pies and jam which Missus managed to make, in spite of the sugar ration. It was made with less than usual but some added apple helped to set it. Certainly not for keeping, but then there were five of us and it would soon be eaten up.

Some time after this Margaret decided to leave. Boss applied for another girl to take her place and a very nice girl came called Jean. She had been working on another farm and wanted a change. She also came from London, like Freda, but was not a cockney. We were to become great friends and kept in touch for a long time after I had left the farm myself.

Sometimes there was mist in the mornings. Then when the sun came through it shone on the spiders' webs which laced the hedges making them sparkle. Occasionally after a clear night there would be a white frost and it was nippy getting the cows in in the morning, but after breakfast the sun would be quite warm and soon clear it away.

Boss, Fred and Freda were busy ploughing the stubble and some grass fields ready for planting seed corn for the next year's crop. It was essential to get it planted while the weather was dry. After ploughing they were cultivating, rolling and harrowing over and again to get the ground flat. The fields were planted differently each year so that a grass one would now have wheat and a wheat one either dredge corn or left for roots.

Quite a few of the cows were calving now so there was a lot of milking to do. The idea was to hopefully get them to do so in the autumn when they would give quite a lot of milk and then in the spring, when they went out to fresh grass, they would have another 'flush'. It didn't always work, depending on when they had held to the bull. Although

80

a lot calved at this time, others did so at infrequent intervals. Some of the heifers that were coming in had a difficult calving owing to an outsize calf. If Boss couldn't cope, then the vet had to be called in to help. They couldn't be left too long or the calf would die. There were a few sleepy calves born which wouldn't suck their mothers and then I had to spend a lot of time mornings and afternoons holding them up and putting the teat in their mouths to encourage them to get on with it. Very often the mother would fidget around making it even more difficult. One had to learn patience and I can only remember one casualty when it must have been that the calf had something wrong with it from birth. Now that a lot of the cows were calving Bob was collecting a new lot of babies to look after, to add to the stragglers which had come in during the summer. So the yard work began to increase.

In the autumn there were many farm sales. Farmers with well-known pedigree herds would sell off surplus animals which they had bred. Boss decided to go to one and came back with a lovely yearling bull to bring on for use in his own herd. He was put in a pen on his own and was quiet and friendly. He was like a young prince. We knew he had cost a lot of money and we used to look at him in awe, when helping to feed and clean him out. He wouldn't be ready to go with the heifers for some months and had to be carefully looked after to keep him in good condition. He was allowed out in the yard for exercise while being cleaned out and frisked around nosing over the pens at the other calves, but was no trouble to get back in. We just rattled some calf cake in a bucket and that did the trick. " 'Ee be a gud in," said Bob and that summed it up.

Soon after this Boss said it was time to get the potatoes up. Fred being experienced, was going to plough them out and us others pick them up in buckets which, when full,

81

we would tip into sacks. When there were enough for a trailer load Boss and Freda would take them back to the farm, Fred helping after he'd ploughed up a few rows. They were to be cleared up as we went, so that there were none lying around overnight in case of any frost.

It seemed pleasant enough to start with. The sun was first warm after an early mist. George and I walked up the adjacent rows but I soon got left behind. Although I'd been used to carrying buckets of milk, potatoes weighed a lot heavier. The buckets were quite large and it was as much as I could do to carry one three parts full. Inevitably George would reach the end of the row before me, but came back to help finish mine off so we could start again together. I think it made him feel a bit superior that I wasn't quite up to his standard after all. For myself, I was jolly glad to let him help. I'd never wanted to be super woman, only reasonably able to cope.

After a while we both slowed down. Bending up and down my back was killing me and while not saying anything I saw George rub his occasionally. We carried on until dinner-time and then again in the afternoon. Once more I was thankful that soon George and I would be able to leave the field and go to get the cows in for milking while Boss, Fred and Freda would stay and clear up until tea-time. They would finish before us, as we wouldn't be working in the field evenings now, but I preferred the afternoon change in the cowshed.

After harvesting the potatoes we had a couple of weeks doing odd jobs. Then it was time for the mangolds. They had to be pulled, have the tops twisted or cut off, and piled in heaps. Fred and George being old hands got on pulling and twisting away like mad. I tried to copy but not only could I not pull some of them, twisting seemed impossible. Boss took pity on me and gave me an old knife to cut off the tops. I found that a good kick would loosen some of them, as they were growing half out of the ground. However, I then stubbed my toe, so I had to go much more carefully after that. Needless to say I soon got left behind. I didn't really care. I was doing my best and for once the men didn't make any snide remarks. In fact, Fred actually consoled me, "Thee's 'ave tu git un the way," he said. I doubted I'd ever get in the way of it — strong wrists and fingers were needed. Still, I didn't say so and plodded on.

After we'd pulled a few rows, Freda came into the field with the tractor and trailer. It made a break as we loaded up the heaps. When the trailer was full, her and Boss went back with it to the farm to unload and we others were back on the beat. We did about a third that first day. While Boss, George and I went milking in the afternoon, Fred and Freda cleared up the remaining heaps, leaving the rest for action the next day.

Overnight it rained, but had stopped by the morning. Up in the mangold field the ground was slippery and so were the mangolds. The leaves, being wet, were difficult to twist or cut and altogether it was a messy business. Here, too, in the middle of the field, they were bigger and I found I had to use both hands to throw every one into the heap. I gradually became wet and covered in mud, as I clutched at the monsters and more than once skidded over the discarded leaves. There were even more hazards ahead.

It was fairly easy to load them onto the bottom of the trailer. I just picked up the small ones, leaving the men to the others. Alas, as the load became higher, some would roll off. Not only that, as we were loading up each side, we had to dodge one coming over the top, or get a hefty whack. I was the first culprit; throwing up the small ones they went over more easily. I was not looking up to see, until a shout from Fred, "Dust wanna kill I?" came over. After this, I

83

was more careful but didn't escape myself. One walloped me as I bent over. "Bes let thic du," said Fred after a lot began to roll off. There was a limit to the number which could be safely put up.

During the day we had showers of rain which didn't help. Clad now in a heavy mac it was difficult to work, although having put on a Land Army hat I felt safer from a knockout blow from any more mis-directed mangolds.

The next day, after more rain, conditions were even worse. We went on pulling and heaping but they had to give up any carting after the trailer got stuck in mud. It was all hands to the wheels as the tractor chugged away trying to pull it out. Suddenly, with a lurch, it moved. We all dodged as mangolds came hurtling off. The tractor went on, leaving us to dig them out of the mud and pile them up. As we made the heaps we now covered them over with leaves as they would have to be left until the ground was dry enough to cart. This was to protect them in case the weather changed and there were frosts. We finished pulling and left the field.

For a few days I went off with George to do some ditching. Fred and Freda were bringing in loads of loose straw from the base of old ricks and started to cover up the growing stack of mangolds, which they had already tipped in the rick barton. In the meantime, the weather dried up and then we were able to go back to the field to finish off the job.

Although the weather was now dry it had turned cold. Uncovering the heaps of the leaves they felt icy, as were the mangolds. I had to keep rubbing my numbed hands. George, as usual, seemed immune. It was still very precarious moving the loads. The tractor and trailer had made ruts when the ground was soft and these had hardened. Although Fred drove very slowly and tried to steer a course around them, inevitably he would have to weave over a section to get through the gate. We made smaller loads, but still some of the mangolds fell off as the trailer lurched along. Progress was slow, as we had to pick a lot of them up again. We didn't finish that day and that night there was a frost. This made it a colder job than ever. Going in to milking was even more attractive. The cows udders were at least warm. However, eventually we cleared the field and 'mangolling' was over for another year.

Chapter Eleven

OUT AND ABOUT

Life became pleasant once more. The weather turned mild and damp, but there were sunny intervals. After the routine jobs I went down with George to cut out the meadows. There were gulleys across them which would be flooded the next spring to bring on the grass. During the summer, however, they got trodden in by the cows in places. Our job was to renew them. George had a long turf knife and as he went chopping wedges out along the sides, I followed, lifting them on to the edge and patting them firmly down. There was not much conversation. George was a man of few words. I wondered what he thought about all day. He only seemed interested in cows. I was dreaming of a young airman I'd met on the bus on my last weekend off. It seemed he lived in the village near my home and was going there on leave. We spent a nice Saturday afternoon at the cinema in our local town. I had also gone to his home on the Sunday for tea. We agreed to write but he was posted and, as it happened, later on we lost touch.

It was now well into autumn and time to put the clocks back one hour. We didn't have to change ours. It was a relief to be on the same wave length as everyone else. It made life a lot easier. Consequently we girls thought we'd

86

plan a little break. Jean and I still had our alternate week-ends off, so as we were not very busy, we persuaded Boss to let us have one weekend together. Then, with Freda, we were going to London. Their homes were there, but I had only been as a child with my father on business once or twice and then only for a day. I couldn't remember much of that, so I was eagerly looking forward to the trip. I felt a bit apprehensive when I remembered what Freda had said about the air-raids and bombed streets, but I wouldn't be on my own and maybe there wouldn't be any raids while we were there.

We went off soon after milking on a Saturday morning and arrived in London for lunch. There was still food of a sort to be had at Lyon's Corner House. After a meal, Jean and Freda took me on a tour around to see some of the famous sights. We were dressed up in our going out Land Army uniforms and soon became the butt of some children in Hyde Park. Presumably they'd never seen anyone like us girls in breeches, but we didn't bother about their giggling.

I was surprised to see the trees were all black, never having been in this part of London before. We spent the evening with Freda's parents in central London. As they only had a flat, we camped on the living-room floor. It all seemed exciting, but in the night I was really scared when the air-raid siren went. Freda being used to it, only said that we'd best get under the table. It was before the real blitz and people didn't go to the air-raid shelters much. Whether there was one near there I didn't know and later on her parents moved away from London. The all clear sounded and we slept till 5 am when the city woke up. The noise seemed terrific after our quiet country life.

After breakfast we again went sightseeing. There hadn't been much damage there as yet, but apparently there was some elsewhere as she had told us. Later we went out to

Jean's home in Hampstead for lunch. Then we had a pleasant walk in the afternoon on the heath.

After tea we went back to the city to catch the train home. It had been a very nice break but I didn't think I would like to live in London, especially during the war.

The next day Boss said we were going threshing and soon after breakfast a steam engine arrived outside the farm pulling a threshing machine. There were a couple of men, one driving the steam engine and one on the thresher. Boss directed them up to the cornfield then took Fred, George, Freda and Jean with him, and also a tractor and trailer with a load of sacks.

As it was my turn doing the yard work, I was to go up after dinner. They had stripped off the thatch and already started threshing in the morning. It needed a lot of hands to keep going. Even old Shep had been asked to come and help. The thresher was by the first rick and George and Freda had been on the rick and pitching the sheaves over on it. Mr X and Mr Y had cut the strings and fed the loose corn stalks into the drum. Shep, with Jean's help, had already started a rick from the straw which was coming out one end; at the other were some sacks of corn and one fixed ready to be filled. Boss had been coping with this job. On one side chaff, which was the corn husks all beaten and powdery, had blown out into a heap and Fred had been clearing it back.

When we all started again in the afternoon the others went on with their various jobs, except Fred, who went to help Boss with shifting the corn and loading on to the trailer. I was detailed to take over from him on the chaff. Of all the jobs I had on the farm it was certainly the worst. The dust not only blew all over you, in your eyes and up your nose making you sneeze, but it was difficult to keep it clear with a hay fork as it was soft and light and I kept sinking in the heap. It was also very dirty. Fred came round to see how I was getting on and laughed.

"Thee's u'll make a gud swip."

As usual, George, Jean and I were excused for milking in the afternoon while the others carried on, albeit at a much slower pace, as Fred had to go on the corn rick on his own, while Freda helped with the dust.

Back at the farm when I went in for a cuppa and a quick face wash, looking in the bathroom mirror I could see what Fred had meant. My face was filthy and bits were in my eyebrows. I was glad I'd worn a hat and jacket. At night when I took off my socks which had heaps of chaff in as well, my ankles and feet were also black. Freda was also filthy.

Next day Boss thought we ought to have a change round, so Jean went on the dust and I helped Shep to make the straw rick. It wasn't easy. As it came churning out of the thresher, I had to grab it and pass it back to Shep. It was very slippery standing on the edge of the rick which was now getting quite high and I slid about. Bits of straw also stuck in my socks and scratched my ankles. It was better than the dust. However, the worst moments were yet to come.

Later on we had to use the elevator to carry the straw up to the rick as it was too high to pitch it on. Fred took over grabbing the straw and pushing it in the elevator, while I was still up on the rick and passed it back to Shep. Shep had brought his dog, a little wire haired terrier. She kept running around and yapping and getting under everyone's feet. I asked him what had he bothered to bring her for.

"Thee's 'ull sun know," he said.

The corn rick was nearly finished and looking down I saw rats and mice scampering about. The terrier went wild and sunk her teeth into some of them, while Boss beat up others with a stick. Jean let out a shriek as one came running round in the dust, dropped her fork and ran.

e

I didn't blame her. I was glad I was up out of the way or I would have done the same. Shep snorted and paused to take a pinch of snuff.

"Was 'er du thit fer, silly creturs wimmen."

I defended her. "I shall run too if I'm on the dust at the end of the next rick," I told him.

" 'Ave a bit o' thic snoff, 'twu'll du ee gud." He offered me the snuff tin. I'd tried it before when I was helping him make thatch and wasn't going to try again. I declined politely.

Meanwhile there was now a huge pile of straw to move. Down below the excitement had stopped. The rick was finished and the rats and mice had all disappeared except for several dead ones. The terrier sat by them exhausted but triumphant. Jean came back and we all finished clearing up. Shep roofed in the straw rick. The corn was loaded to take back to the farm and we all helped shovel the chaff into bags. Then Mr X and Mr Y moved the thresher to start on the next rick, which we would begin after lunch.

It took a few days to finish. We had been threshing the winter oats, some of which would be sold but some left for rolling to feed the cows in the mixture with linseed or cotton cake and dried sugar-beet. The men departed with the thresher and steam engine to another farm. They would come back in the new year for another session with the wheat.

The days were getting short. Boss and Freda went out in the fields first preparing the ground and then planting winter oats and wheat. Much of my time between milking was spent helping to bring in the hay for the cows. I would go with Fred and the tractor and trailer to a hayrick. He would pull off the straw thatch on one corner. Then with a large hay knife slice out slabs of hay, carrying them on his head he then dumped them on the trailer. It was my job to poke it round and make the load. I wondered if that was the reason he always wore his cap on backwards. The peak protecting his neck and stopping the hay going down his back. Old Bob wore his the same so maybe that's why he did as well.

Back at the farm we unloaded the hay into the bays at the end of the cow stalls. We spread some in the cribs after milking evenings ready for them coming in in the morning. Also some cow cake mixture. They were rationed with this according to their milk yield.

We also went to the root field where the kale was now tall and thick with leaves. Fred would chop it down with a hook and we had to load it on the cart with a prong. It was difficult to do. I couldn't seem to get hold of the stalks. They slivered about and I was lucky to pick up one. Then the leaves were usually wet and I'd get a shower of water all over me. If there had been a frost it would be icy lumps instead. When the cart was full, Fred would drive it out to the field where the cows were. Usually I was on the cart and supposed to distribute the kale as Fred drove around. There was not much grass and when the cows saw us coming, they would mill around delighted. They would grab and pull some of it off. As it started to go, the rounded stalks under my feet would roll around and I had a job to keep my balance. I dug in the prong and held on, letting them pull off what they could reach. Then I shovelled off the rest as best I could, sometimes falling over and getting very wet. Fred thought it very funny and grinned all over his face.

In the evenings we girls would change and sit by the fire either reading, knitting or chatting. Sometimes we went into town on our bikes to the pictures but it wasn't easy to see the way with dimmed lights and the blackout everywhere. The others occasionally went to a dance in town. Then Freda found herself a soldier boyfriend and we didn't see much of her after work.

On Armistice Day there was to be a parade in the local town. We were informed by HQ it was our duty to go and join in with other girls in the district. It would be nice to meet some of our own kind, though where they were working we had no idea. We certainly hadn't come across any girls in the surrounding farms where we were.

So we duly arrived, clad in our best uniforms. Lined up by the barracks just going into town were a few bandsmen, about a dozen soldiers, half a dozen airmen and three nurses and that was it. No sign of any Land Army girls. Someone said it was time to go, so off went the band followed by the others, us bringing up the rear. People stared at us. I don't suppose there had been any land girls in any previous parades. They probably thought we were not the forces as they knew them. It was a very mild sunny day and by the time we had marched to the war memorial we were sweltering in our thick jumpers, breeches and topcoats, and wished we'd stayed at home.

After the service, one of the nurses told me that it was voluntary for them to go. I suspected it was for us too, only we hadn't known. I learnt later that there was a Land Army hostel the other side of the town, with a number of girls going out working on different farms. Obviously none of them had bothered to turn up.

Chapter Twelve

FULL CIRCLE

Christmas came. The two days holiday were treated as a weekend and only essential work done. Freda and I were allowed time off as we lived not so far away, but Jean stayed to help the men. I enjoyed being home with my family and the time passed too quickly. In the New Year the weather turned cold and we had a little snow.

Boss said it was time to keep the cows in by night. Some of the fields were very wet and they could not be used as they would get trampled up too much. It meant keeping the cows in the few fields that were near the farm by day. We had to give them hay twice a day now that they stayed in at night. As it took a time, Boss, Freda and Fred started bringing in the loads of hay. They also brought in some straw for bedding, which was put in the other end bays. When the kale had all been eaten, there were mangolds to chop up to give the cows with their cow cake. This was put in the cribs. Fred would bring a load into the barn, where they had to be put into the chopper and ground up. It was very hard work to turn the handle and being round they often became stuck.

It was dark when we started in the morning but lovely and warm in the cowsheds. The cows would contentedly munch away at the hay, mangolds and cake while we cleared back the overnight dung and then got on with the milking. After breakfast, washing up the milking machine, cleaning and washing out the sheds and putting down straw for bedding and hay for the evening, took nearly all day for both Jean and I, Bob and George. Then there were Bob's calves and the bulls to feed and water.

Pixie hoods were very much in fashion in those days for cold weather. Usually woollen, they had a peak at the top and tied under the chin. They were very warm and I had a red one for work, instead of the Land Army hat which would blow off in a wind.

In the morning, while putting in hay for the cows, I would get very hot and gradually discard hat and jacket. I was in the habit of putting them on the bar near the hay end. One day, when we had finished, I went to collect them before putting on my white coat for milking. The hat was missing — I searched everywhere over and under the tumbled hay, but it was nowhere to be found. I looked in the nearest cribs and poked in the hay there much to the cows' disgust. They snorted and tossed their heads. It wasn't there. I thought Fred had been playing a trick on me and had hidden it. He always liked to tease, but now he assured me:

"Fer certain un o' thic cows ad eaten un, they loiks thic colour."

I stared at him incredulously, I just didn't believe it.

" 'T'is roit," he said. "Thic uns 'ull eat any 'ole thing." He then went on to tell me the tale of what happened once when Missus put her washing on the line in the orchard. Some of the calves had been let out there and they chewed off the legs of her, well, "the'se 'ull naw." He kept a straight face, although there was a wicked look in his eye.

I decided he was having me on.

"Corse 'er niver puts it ut ther when they be ther now,"

he said, so that I had no way of knowing if it were true, short of asking her. I didn't think that would be very tactful and dropped the subject. However, after several days of looking around in case my pixie hat had been carried off in some hay, I still didn't find it, and when the bay was empty of hay it wasn't underneath or anywhere. I asked Bob if he had seen it, but all he said was "Naw arrh", instead of his usual 'aw arrh'.

I reluctantly wondered if Fred was right and the remains of my hat were being digested through one of the cows' stomachs. I would have thought it would give it indigestion, at least. The ones tied up nearest the hay bay remained well and I gave up. Bulls were supposed to go mad seeing a red rag, but cows liking to chew red pixie hats was beyond me. I bought myself another one, blue this time, and made sure I didn't leave it anywhere near them.

Some time after I remembered the incident of the spring before, when we were moving heifers and they had gone in a garden and started chewing the washing. Years later, having forgotten all about any of this, I put some washing on a line in an orchard where there were cows. They immediately made a beeline for it and started chewing anything they could reach. Needless to say 'I never put moin 'ut ther agin' unless there were no animals around.

In the autumn Fred and Freda had shifted most of the dung from the heaps at the end of the cowsheds. They had loaded it onto the dung carts and these were pulled by the horses. They led them out to some of the fields and tipped it out in piles, then spread it around with prongs. These fields had consequently been ploughed, cultivated and sown with winter cereals. Now, at the end of winter, massive new heaps of dung had accumulated. So they started to move this out to those fields to be used for spring corn sowing and the roots ground.

Sometimes in the afternoon, if I had finished the other jobs, Boss would send me out to help spread the muck around. Some of it which had been out a while was easy to cope with. As it had rotted, the straw in it broke up and it flaked as I shook it off the prong. When this was all used and the fresh dung came out it was different altogether. It was sticky and wet and the straw tangled round making it difficult to pick up. Then when I flung it some would flop back and I'd get blobs on my face or in my eye. It was hard work but kept anyone doing it warm.

On a day when I'd been cleaning out cowsheds and spreading muck in the field, I would feel life was one long battle with dung and I certainly smelt like a heap until I'd washed and changed in the evening. It was supposed to be healthy and I did develop a rosy colour which I'd never had before.

During the summer heat I had become very thin but now I had plumped up and began to look like a real country girl, so Fred said: "The'se loik a prupper mide nu." And Bob, who was there, said:

"Aw arrh!"

For some days I'd had a spot on my wrist which irritated. Apart from rubbing it I hadn't really taken much notice, until it started to get bigger, in a round, about the size of a farthing, which was similar in size to a penny nowadays. Soon it seemed to be as big as an old half penny. I still was not bothered. At home, on a weekend visit, I mentioned it to my parents who recognised it as ringworm and advised me to see the doctor.

Back at the farm I cycled into the local town to the evening surgery. The doctor confirmed their diagnosis and gave me some white ointment to rub in. He remembered me from the scabies days and remarked that I seemed to pick up skin complaints. However, he assured me that the ringworm would soon disappear.

It did not, but gradually got bigger, still going round in a circle, eating away the skin as it went.

I returned to the doctor who then gave me some evil-smelling black ointment which he said would certainly do the trick this time. Not so. It had no effect and I now had a ring half way around my wrist.

I had been wearing a bandage with the ointment to keep it from smearing my blouse cuff. "Wot be up wid thee?" asked Fred. I told him and asked him how did he think I'd got it. One or two calves had had small patches of ringworm, but had been cleared with vets' treatment. I hadn't been near them anyway like Bob had and he hadn't caught it.

"Wull maybe tis on t'riles," Fred said.

I presumed he meant on the wooden railings round the calf pens. Probably the calves had rubbed against the pens and I had then brushed against them. As the doctor said, I was liable to skin complaints.

"Bes sid to it wid oink," continued Fred.

I couldn't believe my ears. "Did you say ink?" I said, and gave him a penetrating look to see if he was having me on again.

No, his face was dead straight and not even a sign of a twinkle in his eye. "Aw arrh," he said, using Bob's favourite expression. " 'Tis wots rate fer thic un."

For a day or two I thought this over. Maybe it was an old country cure. The doctor's ointment hadn't done any good. So I decided to try it. I had writing ink as we used it for letters in those days. Gingerly I patted some all around my wrist and re-bandaged it. I didn't mention this to Boss, Missus or the other girls. They knew I had been to the doctor with it, but I thought they might think I was mad to paint my wrist with ink.

I certainly must have been. It didn't do any good, except

to make my arm sorer than ever and the ringworm went gaily round and round. I decided to clean it off quick, but it took several washes and my arm became really raw. It was now going up my hand and almost up to my elbow.

On my next visit home my parents insisted on my seeing their doctor in the village near my home. He recognised me and said, "Aren't you the girl I advised not to join the Land Army?" I said I was, but assured him that I was fine except for this little trouble of ringworm. He looked at my arm and then at me. "Sorry," he said, "it's not a little problem, I'm afraid, you'll have to go to the hospital for treatment. I'll give you an appointment card. When you've been to the hospital you must not return to work but report back to me."

Few people had telephones and we were no exception, so I had to ring the farm from the telephone box by the village post office to explain the situation. Then I took the bus to the local town and made my way to the hospital. Arriving, I was shown into out-patients, where several other people were waiting, some with plaster on an arm or leg, making their complaints obvious, but I wondered what had brought the others.

I didn't have long to contemplate when I was swished off by a nurse to see a skin specialist. He looked at my arm, but tutted that I should have come before and on no account was I to go back to the farm until it was completely healed. Then he gave the nurse some instructions and I was away to the treatment room.

Well I had had a poisoned finger, a septic wound on my knee, a couple of boils and a few other things requiring painful treatment in the past, but when the nurse painted all over my raw arm with carbolized iodine I nearly fainted. She was very kind, "it had to be done," she said, "now we'll cool it down," and proceeded to slap ice cold cream all over. What a relief. Then she bandaged me all up. She said my arm would be stiff for a while and it was best to rest it in a sling. However, that was not the end of it. Giving me a small bottle of carbolized iodine and a brush she instructed me to paint it several times a day around all the edge of the affected skin on my arm. This was to stop the ringworm spreading any more. Compared to nowadays, treatment then was really punitive.

I duly reported back to the doctor and was put on the panel as it was then called. He gave me a certificate to draw some health benefit. I was to call in on Mondays for renewals.

Having been so busy working nearly all the time on the farm, I felt very much at a loose end at home. Until now I hadn't done much sewing. It was suggested that I get out the sewing machine and have a go at making a dress. Clothes and material were then on coupons. We had to surrender some for our Land Army uniform, but were allowed to keep some for other items like nightwear etc. I had a few left, so I went off to the market in the local town where there were still stalls selling materials. They were in very short supply in the shops and even the market had a limited choice. I managed to get a nice woollen remnant and a pattern. It was only just enough for a short sleeved dress.

So, with a little help from mother, I launched into making my own clothes. I was then promised a sewing machine for my 21st birthday in a year's time. Meanwhile I could use the one at home when I came back. Eventually I had to settle for a new second-hand one, purchased from a friend, as by that time new ones were almost unobtainable and shops had a very limited quota.

Making the dress helped to pass some of the time but I still found it long. I went for walks in the fields and woods around home. Spring was beginning. There were a few primroses out and other signs of new life. I faithfully treated my arm with iodine but although the ringworm seemed to stop spreading my whole arm looked an awful mess.

When I went to the doctor he just looked at it and said it would improve. In the end it was several weeks later that I was allowed to go back to work. I still had to be careful as I now had pink new skin which hadn't toughened up at all and I had to wear long sleeves for protection.

On returning to the farm I found quite a change. Boss and Missus had decided they would no longer accommodate us girls and we were to be billeted out. I was to live with Bob and his wife and the others were found lodgings in the village.

I was quite attached to Bob by now and as he and his wife had no family they treated me as one of their own. She did my washing and spoilt me no end. Even so, I missed the others, although we could meet up evenings it wasn't the same as being together like we were before.

The cows had gone out to grass and we started spring cleaning the cowsheds. We were about to begin the whole year's cycle once again.

Whether it was being away from the farm so long, or moving into digs away from the other girls, I didn't seem to be able to settle down at all. It had been a good year on the whole. Hard work hadn't hurt me and we'd had some happy times with a lot of laughs. Also some painful ones as well, in more senses than one.

I thought it all over, again and again. I was no longer a novice. I reckoned I had become quite a competent dairy maid and not too bad at other jobs. I had learnt an awful lot, but there were other animals and aspects of farming of which I'd had no experience. Then there was the prospect of more double trouble with our clocks not being put forward in the summer.

At last I knew it was time to make a move to a different scene and pastures new.